GLEANINGS

GLEANINGS
Sister Bertrande Meyers,
Daughter of Charity
An Anthology of Published Articles and Addresses

EDITED BY
Sister Beatrice Brown,
Daughter of Charity

An Exposition-Testament Book

EXPOSITION PRESS   HICKSVILLE, NEW YORK

FIRST EDITION

Contents

Preface

With her usual thoroughness, she had left us—we found at Sister Bertrande's death—"bound hand and foot" with prohibitions against any attempt, or even success, at writing her biography. Yet, more and more, we her closest friends, struggled ambivalently—to *have* the biography at hand, and yet honestly to deny having written it.

Finally, we discovered thirty or so original published articles. Arranged in alphabetical order, they were fairly impressive by reason of the wide range of the subject matter. A chronological arrangement accentuated the fact that they were "occasional." Occasion after occasion drew a statement from her; rarely trite, often convincing.

Reading the paper today and recalling the enthusiastic response of audiences some years ago convinces the editor that few, if any, audiences remained indifferent to Sister Bertrande's opinions. But she hungered for the challenge of those who, loving her none the less, could say, "I must differ on this point, Sister." Regardless of time or place, she said often, "Let's pursue this . . . : I want to understand your point of view—especially, if I'm wrong." The lesson was clear: I, too, must needs seek the truth, and yield to none.

The other fact which must be considered is that Sister Bertrande was not assigned time from her administrative duties in which to write—excepting for her dissertation, *The Education of Sisters,* the format of which required time and travel.

The principle governing the choice for this anthology is fairly complex: made clear through the invitations—men's groups, family groups, MSW's, librarians, teen-agers, National Association of

Social Workers, the National Catholic Education Association, Association for Higher Education, North Central Association and related groups. Obviously, the editor is tempted to give a sample of everything, producing the impression of shallowness . . .

There were, indeed, two outstanding subjects, which more and more pervaded most of Sister's writing: teaching and religion. Perhaps she returned at the end of her career to the product whose process she had guided in her earlier books—the well educated Sister, effective—even joyous in her job.

Dan Herr in one of his pithy paragraphs from *Overview* supports the opinions expressed here by the editor.

Sister Bertrande Meyers is one of the pioneers in the study of religious life in the light of modern conditions. In the autumn issue of *Thought,* Sister Bertrande objects to the current question "What is wrong with the religious life," believing that a more pertinent question is "What ails religious life?" She sees a distinction between "being wrong and being sick," and believes that only the second question is worthy of discussion. In her opinion, few will dispute that "the religious life is ailing," and she lists these symptoms: "a marked restlessness among Sisters, many defections, much confusion brought on by uncertainty and ambivalence toward changes in the Church, disdain for the past, instability, resentment of authority, lack of trust in anyone but their peers, a continuous challenge of the validity of the 'call' of vocation." For some the pace of change is coming too fast; for others too slowly; and for many the emphasis has been on details rather than on major issues. Among the major issues she sees endangering the vitality of contemporary religious life are the need for a stern and forthright reappraisal in terms of corporate poverty; the lack of specially prepared and educated mistresses of novices; and the lack of courageous leadership." Sister concludes: "It might well be that pervading friendship, understood, appreciated, and cultivated in religious communities would prove to be the healing agent in the three 'ailing' areas."

A more formal envoy is the letter quoted from the Apostolic Delegate, E. Vagnozzi. Unsolicited, it came to Sister Bertrande, who did not divulge the contents. But we have nonetheless chosen it for recommendation to today's reader.

Apostolic Delegation
United States of America
3339 Massachusetts Avenue
Washington, D.C. 20008

16 March 1967

Sister Bertrande Meyers, D.C.
Daughters of Charity
7800 Natural Bridge Road
St. Louis, Missouri

Dear Sister Bertrande:

Your article, "Sisters . . . Isn't It About Time" in the issue of Ave Maria for March 4th is one of the most discerning and well-balanced analyses that I have recently seen. It reflects a mature religious life of your own and a keen appreciation of the values that are important in it. Obviously you have not been stampeded by the destructive criticism of those who have been so vocal in the press and on television.

You understand the vistas open to Sisters today without prejudice to their basic vocation. As you note, this is clearly defined in the documents of the Council. I might cite that on religious renewal: "The members of each community should recall above everything else that by their profession of the evangelical counsels they have given answer to a divine call to live for God alone, not only by dying to sin but also by renouncing the world. They have handed over their entire lives to God's service in an act of special consecration which is deeply rooted in their baptismal consecration and which provides an ampler manifestation of it." (N.5)

I would encourage you to pursue this same theme in other articles. You will not only be defending the truth but you will bring inestimable consolation to the legion of dedicated religious women in this country who do not have your ability to articulate the feelings they share with you.

With cordial regards and best wishes, I am
Sincerely yours in Christ,

(Signed)   + E. Vagnozzi
                     Apostolic Delegate

So, we confidently offer our GLEANINGS.

Sister Beatrice Brown
Daughter of Charity
Editor

Acknowledgements

Grateful acknowledgement is given to the following publications in which the articles in this anthology first appeared:

The Journal of Religious Instruction, in which "A Cause in Christ" first appeared in 1943.

Vital Speeches of the Day, in which "The New Excellence" first appeared in the June 15, 1960 issue, Vol. 26, No. 17; and in which "Raise Your Voice—Cast Your Vote" first appeared in the August 15, 1967 issue, Vol. 33, No. 21.

Thought, in which "Four Stories of Flannery O'Connor" first appeared in the Autumn 1962 issue, Vol. 37, No. 146; and in which "Who Is Sick Among Us?" first appeared in the Autumn 1966 issue, Vol. 41, No. 162.

Esprit, in which Sister Bertrande Meyers' contribution to "Flannery O'Connor—A Tribute" first appeared in the Winter 1964 issue, Vol. 8, No. 1, pp. 13-14.

Sister Formation Bulletin, in which "The Place of Religious in Social Work" first appeared in the Summer 1957 issue.

Ave Maria, in which "Sisters, Isn't It About Time?" first appeared in the March 4, 1967 issue. Reprinted with permission, *Ave Maria,* Notre Dame, Indiana, March 4, 1967.

Sisters Today, in which "Fire, Flood, Earthquake—Sursum Corda, Sisters!" first appeared in the June 1967 issue, Vol. 38, No. 10.

Daughter of Charity, in which "Good-bye, Sister Zoe" first appeared in the Summer 1967 issue, Vol. 5, No. 4.

1

A Cause in Christ

"I find no cause in Him." Flat and final, the words came from the lips of Pilate, a summation and a dismissal of his relations with Christ. He refused to investigate Christ's claim to kingship, and thus rejected His authority; he remained indifferent to the nature of the truth that Christ proclaimed, and thus rejected His doctrine. After this double rejection, what could follow but the declaration: "I find no cause in Him."

These words, so often cited in palliation of Pilate's conduct, are in reality its condemnation. They are the key to Pilate's character, and consequently to his guilt. To him, Christ is at best "innocent"—synonymous here with innocuous. He finds in Him no cause for condemnation, but neither does he find in Him a cause for dedication. He has seen Jesus and conversed with Him; He has studied His actions and His attitude. But he is not moved to proclaim Him wise, august, powerful, divine—no, only "innocent." He finds in Him no cause to love, to venerate, to worship. No cause to proclaim himself the friend of Christ, to strike a blow in His defense. No cause for which to sacrifice position, reputation, life itself. Pilate finds no cause in Him—in Christ, the Ultimate Cause of every cause!

By some scriptural commentators, Pilate has been handled quite gently. Tertullian speaks of him as one who rejected Christ but who would have accepted Christianity, while the Abyssinian Church has found for this weak-willed man a place in its martyrology. But the Catholic Church—One, Holy, Roman and Apostolic—holds with neither heresy nor schism; it insistently demands that its members shall find a cause in Christ. Fortu-

1

nately, in the educational field, example precedes precept, for those upon whom rests largely the task of education—Priests and Sisters—have found in Christ a cause of utter dedication. Do we always follow up this initial, vocational advantage?

• • •

. . . Should not, . . . the majority of those graduated from our Catholic schools go out with a fixed ideal of Christ as a model and a leader, steadfast in the conviction that Christ is a cause for which to live and to die? Catholic schools are sometimes accused of a lack of patriotism. Our easy answer to that is the thirty-one percent of Catholics enlisted in the defense of our country. Is it out of place to ask ourselves if we are doing as well by the Church, Christ's Mystical Body, as we are doing by our country? Graduates from our Catholic schools and colleges who are defaulters on their national obligations are, thank God, rare. Did every Catholic student have a Christian character formed within him, defaulters to Christ would be still more rare. Could we not thoughtfully and profitably compare the routine "Be proud that you are an American" of the civics class, with the not infrequently heard "Never be ashamed that you are a Catholic" of the religion class? This "Never be ashamed that you are a Catholic" may well be the *terminus a quo* of many a Pilate-patterned pupil.

• • •

TEACHING THE TEACHER

First, in regard to herself, Faith teaches the religious teacher, that she is divinely commissioned to carry on her work—she has "the mission to educate." It teaches her that she has at hand the "tools," physical, mental and moral, needed for the work. It teaches her that she can say of herself, even as Christ said of Himself: "I am not alone, but I and the Father that sent Me"; she is but the intermediary agent between God and the soul of each of her pupils.

Second, in regard to her pupils, Faith teaches the teacher that the body with its physical powers is united to a soul endowed with reason and free will; that as a creature, he is responsible to a Creator—a responsibility that imposes obedience to the Creator's laws, made known to him through the Church, depository of divine authority. It teaches her that the Catholic pupil with whom she deals has free access, through prayer and the sacraments, to supernatural grace, thus placing him definitely beyond the slavery of purely mechanistic behavior. It teaches her that, through grace, the pupil can be raised from the vassalage of the ignoble to the sonship of the noble—from lawless freedom to the liberty of the law.

Furnished by Faith with these certainties, the religious teacher faces serenely, but with no underestimation of either the difficulty or the sacredness of her task, the duty of so shaping the character of her pupils that Catholic ideals will dominate their lives and Catholic habits control their conduct. Here is the dual work of instructing in the principles of faith and training in the practice of virtue. If she succeeds in both, her pupils will go forth with characters cast in the same Christian mould that has successfully shaped and formed character for the past two thousand years.

WHAT IS CHARACTER?

What is character? Imitating the brevity of Revelation, wherein God succinctly defines His divine entity as "I am Who am," we may say, "Character is what you are." This "what you are" is the end product of heredity, environment, ideals, and habits. What is the teacher's part in the formation of her pupils' character? Heredity is fixed. Environment, save as it concerns the hours spent in the classroom, she can influence but indirectly. But ideals and habits, the two factors wherein the mind and the will count most, are hers to work with. How may she work with them? Through the natural and the supernatural—and both are of God.

Religious teachers are not infrequently inclined to minimize the importance of the natural virtues. Accepting as true that "Life here derives its highest value by serving as a preparation for the life to come" we sometimes fail to apply this to a lower and more immediate level, and accept: "A school's greatest temporal value is its preparation for post-school life." In business, social, and economic life, the natural virtues count high for success, and they are the ones that are almost instantly obvious. Politeness, for example, is a public matter; purity, a private one. Honesty may go unquestioned for years, but industry is challenged the first day on the job. Piety is demonstrated in church; punctuality in the place of employment. It may well be that in our zeal for the theological virtues of faith, hope, and charity, we have neglected the sociological virtues of thrift, order, and reliability. Yet, these natural virtues can be idealized and are even more easily made matters of habit than are the supernatural virtues; further, through spiritual motivation, they become supernatural, and thus ramparts of defense against the base and mean are reinforced. Pilate might have found a cause in Christ, had his weak half-faith been bolstered by a strong sense of fair play. Surely it was this building of the supernatural on the natural that Pius XI had in mind when he wrote:

> Christian education takes in the whole aggregate of human life, physical and spiritual, intellectual and moral, individual, domestic and social.[1]

INCULCATION OF IDEALS

The basis of character training is the inculcation of true and worthy ideals. An ideal is, primarily, a thing of the intellect, for "What the mind does not know, the heart cannot yearn for." But if it remains an intellectual abstraction, it no more serves its purpose than does a book that is never read, or a model that is never copied. As Father Hull well says: "There cannot be char-

---

[1]Encyclical, *Christian Education of Youth.*

acter without some ideal, but there can often be an ideal without character."[2] The effective inculcation of an ideal necessitates the presentation by the teacher, and the perception by the pupil, of some trait or quality or person, in a way that stirs to admiration and to imitation. Embodied, ideals vary, so that an ideal is not so much a pattern as it is the material of a pattern. The ideal doctor, the ideal soldier, the ideal citizen, are different and distinct, but each has qualities that make for the ideal; each is brave, each is self-sacrificing, each is thoroughly conversant with his duties. Common ideals do not, therefore, make for regimentation of personality, but they do insure an identity of character, however divergent be the paths of those who hold them.

Our holy Faith is, and will always be, the greatest constructive force the world has ever known for instilling idealism. How easy for us to follow, in the atmosphere of a Catholic classroom, the four essential steps in the inculcation of ideals. First, there is the clear and definite presentation. The teacher need not grope for material. Christ and His teachings, Christian heroes and their actions, reach in an unbroken chain from present to past. In the second step, excitation to imitation, the bond of spiritual relationship works not less readily than does that of race or nation. Our American pupils may passively admire the bravery, skill, devotion, of one of foreign birth, but they are moved to active imitation of a MacArthur, a Lincoln, a Paul Revere. In like manner, Catholic pupils respond instinctively and with a sense of torch-bearing responsibility, to the deeds and lives of their spiritual forebears.

The third step in the inculcation of ideals, that is, the possibility of attainment, is beautifully cared for by the equalizing effect of divine grace. Agnes, Pancratius, Tarcisius, down to the more recent martyrs of Mexico, had access to no more powerful sources of grace than have the Toms and Susies and Walters of the twentieth-century classrooms. It requires neither the previous

---

[2]Hull, S.J., Earnest R. *The Formation of Character* (St. Louis: B. Herder Book Co., 1935), p. 18.

sinning nor the profound science of an Augustine to ask: "Cannot I do what so many thousands of every age and sex have done?" The fourth and last step, environmental opportunity to live up to the elected ideal, is furnished readily enough by life, but frequently it must be pointed out by the teacher. Our Agneses of today face not a lecherous despot, but the no less lecherous movie or magazine. The panthers that beset the boy-saint of the Coliseum have their sleek and slinking counterparts in many places of amusement, in night clubs, in debasing companionship; and Tommy of the Sacred Heart Parish, no less than Tarcisius of Rome, must fight valiantly to keep Christ intact within his breast.

Religion—Christianity—has the unique, because divine, advantage of presenting not an abstract, but a living ideal in the person of Christ. In presenting this Personality, the teacher has the certainty that the "how to attain to it" is essentially secondary, for the Ideal has power Itself to stir the listener to attainment, "for the seed hath life in itself." Here the teacher should humbly keep in mind Father Drinkwater's excellent refutation of the usually accepted "You cannot draw out what you have not put in."[3] It is just what can be done with living things. One "draws out" of a garden plot a lovely flower, whereas one did not "put in" a single brilliant petal, nor bit of green, nor faintest trace of fragrance. No, one "put in" but a colorless seed. The God-given laws of nature, determining the mutual relationship of seed and soil, or organism and environment, worked out their bionomical way. Saint Paul's application of this natural law to the mystery of our bodily resurrection, may be applied by every teacher to the spiritual seed sown by her. "But thou sowest not the body that shall be, but bare green . . . but God giveth it a body as He will; and to every seed, its proper body."[4] Truly, the teacher sows the doctrine, example, and personality of Christ;

---

[3]Drinkwater, F. H. *The Way Into the Kingdom* (London: Burns, Oates and Washbourne, 1927), p. 14.
   [4]1 Cor. 15:37-38.

but according to divine predestination, there springs up the Christ-like athlete, the Christ-like ascetic, the Christ-like soldier, the Christ-like scholar, the Christ-like parent, the Christ-like priest.

Since, then, Christ is "all things to all men," how shall we go about shaping our pupils to the character of Christ? Obviously, no one teacher, no one school, can take in the entire field of desirable character traits. May not we religious teachers learn of the technique used by our spiritual directors in our own spiritual formation? As we know, they give us, not a galaxy of virtues, but some one virtue on which to concentrate, since centuries of success have shown that an earnest, honest, continuous, striving for one virtue, brings many others in its train. This is as effective in mass, as in individual training. Let a school be outstanding for one fine character trait, and the effort to live up to that will round out in its graduates a desirable character. If one of our American universities can be known, and known favorably, for its snobbishness, and another for the length and strength of its drinking bouts, surely a Catholic school can, by consistently striving for one fine thing that will hallmark its graduates, acquire a reputation befitting its Catholic aims.

CHARACTER AND "COFFEE CORA"

A demonstration of something analogous to this is found in one of our American colleges for women, where the foremost and most influential character educator is found, not in the administration office, not in one of its renowned chairs of learning, but in the domestic department: found in the person of a woman who for more than twenty-five years has presided over the coffee urns in the college cafeteria. One would have to search the payroll to find her correct Christian and surname, so thoroughly has the pseudonym "Coffee Cora" displaced them. Cora and her urns have become inseparable parts of a valuable whole. Enormous copper urns are Cora's—after the fashion of such equipment of a quarter of a century ago—and never within the memory of any student have they shone other than as fine-spun gold. From Sunday morning until Saturday night, viewed any time, from any angle, the urns stand flawless and fleckless; and the coffee dispensed from them is as unvarying in its excellent quality as are the urns in their shining appearance.

It took something like four years, or the passing of one generation of college students, for "Coffee Cora's" faithful work at and on those urns to make an impression. . . . "As bright as Cora's urns" was thoroughly understood as either a sarcastic jibe hurled at a dumb student, or a quick compliment tossed to a smart one. With Cora and her urns entering their sixteenth year of shining service, the students found great pride in both. They "belonged" equally with the row of stately elms and the antiquated "Center Building" preserved as a museum. But the urns decidedly "had something" on tree and hall. They were "alive," the person responsible for them could be talked to, questioned, consulted. And that is precisely what the students took to doing.

Their respect for "Coffee Cora" is immense and profound. They deduce from her remarkable fidelity to one task, and the outstanding success she has achieved in it, that this bespeaks in her qualities that make for a wise and prudent adviser on many subjects. The campus-collected tales of "Coffee Cora" have become sacred tradition. These tales deal with both the general and the particular. To the latter classification belongs the anecdote of the saving of Susan B., lovely junior, from a disastrous elopement. Cora's canny warning: "Miss Susie, that boy ain't your grade and he ain't your grind—you two just won't blend," gave preserving pause to the infatuated girl. The general variety of tales tells of countless freshmen, all but sunk in dismissorial waters, stung to the saving "swim on" by Cora's caustic: "Weak coffee and weak people ought to be thrown out." This legendary lore grows daily from the students' "cafeteria consultations" as Cora fills their cups. A "date" is briefly described, and sober attention given to Cora's opinion of him.

The best girl friend has proven disloyal; does Cora advise that she be dropped? That "trig" course is hard sledding; what does Cora think of students who "switch"? The questions are put in anxious sincerity, and her answers accepted as oracular. Why? Because of the students' respect for one who has unfailingly done one thing well. Cora and her coffee urns are a challenge and a symbol which, for a quarter of a century, not one student has escaped. If the menial can be thus metamorphosed, surely the spiritual can be made serviceable.

CONCENTRATION

Had every teacher some one definite character trait in mind, she would use both religious instruction and personal example in a way that would tend to develop that one trait. Setting as her goal, the inculcation of *one* thing, her classes and her conduct would be emphasized in accordance with her goal. For the sake of illustration, let us suppose that a Catholic school decides that the marked trait of its pupils shall be the supernatural virtue of fortitude, presented to the pupils as courage. How can religious instruction and personal example contribute to this goal?

RELIGION'S CONTRIBUTION TO COURAGE

The dogma and doctrine of Christ are the core of religious instruction. Moreover, Christ Himself is the supreme, living ideal, so that unless "learning Christ" and "putting on Christ" are interchangeable terms, our schools fail in their purpose. We educate in Catholicism, but we do not give a Catholic education. To what end doctrine and dogma, if principles and purposes do not follow? Can we present Christ as the ideal of courage in a way to stir to their depths the emotions of youth? To ask that question is to conjure up instantly the picture of Christ as the Valiant Leader, demanding, above all, courage as the badge of discipleship.

The task faced—the redemption of mankind—called for infinite courage. "For the Son of Man came to seek and to save that which was lost." He showed courage in planning: "Going, therefore, teach ye all nations." He showed courage in self-denial: "Jesus fasted forty days and forty nights." He showed courage in presenting the truth: "Will you also go away?" He showed courage in friendship: "Many sins are forgiven her because she hath loved much." He showed courage in facing His enemies: "I am He." He showed courage under false accusation: "Jesus was silent so that Pilate wondered." He showed courage in the denial of all human affections: "Son, behold thy mother." So does the golden thread of courage, divine, yet human and imitable, run through the entire mortal life of our Blessed Lord.

When the heart of youth is emotionally aroused to admiration of such an Ideal, how readily, how eagerly, it turns to imitation. It will be faithful to the discharge of all of its religious duties, privately and publicly, because that requires *courage*. It will refrain from every form, actual or implied, of lying and deceit, because that requires *courage*. It will persevere at the hard and unattractive task, because that requires *courage*. It will take the part of the absent, the weak, and the unpopular, because that requires *courage*. It will keep on in the face of difficulties and prospective failure, because that requires *courage*. It will dominate the low and base impulses of nature, because that requires *courage*.

How fine for a Catholic student to be convinced that it is cowardice, not courage, that leads a Catholic to ignore or to disobey the laws of the Church; that it is weakness, not strength, to tolerate the questionable joke, to condone the suggestive story, to approve the licentious gesture. In after life, as in the class room, such a student will neither welsh nor wince under deserved punishment, but "stand up to it." He will know that it is only the weakling who sulks and mopes over misunderstandings, and that the morally robust accept such things "in stride." For under the leadership of the Divine Exemplar, supplemented by inspirational instruction, with classroom situations continually presenting opportunities for the practice of courage, the desired likeness to Christ has been brought out.

PERSONAL EXAMPLE'S
CONTRIBUTION TO COURAGE

The personal example of the teacher affirms or negates that which she teaches. . . . The teacher who shows Christian self-control in the presence of rude insubordination, strengthens her pupils incalculably in conquering their own sentiments of anger and resentment.

The teacher may also give example of another type of courage, in the equal and absolute application of predetermined penalties for failures, either in studies or in conduct. The very boy or girl who protests most vehemently against this universal enforcement will, as an adult, be the loudest and most sincere in his praise of the teacher who was swayed neither by threats of revolt nor fear of reprisals. Again, the courage of a teacher, who, having made a mistake in an assignment, a statement, or an admonition, says candidly: "I was wrong," is a thing to bring the adolescent to his feet in ringing cheers. And the courage of a teacher, who praises, as superior to her own, the skill or accomplishments of a fellow-teacher, is of fine gold, whose glint and gleam will never be missed by the eagle eye of youth. Happy the pupil who sits under such a one. Times without number, physically, intellectually, socially, morally, will he master his own inclinations and passions because of the example that has so powerfully moulded his character.

And what of the religious teacher herself? Shall her reward be wholly this reflex one? Shall she have only the compensation of having made of her classroom a drill ground for Christ-like characters? This would, indeed, be rich repayment of her labor, and perhaps she would ask no other. But our Blessed Lord will add much more, fulfilling in her regard His promise of "good measure, pressed down and shaken together and running over."[5] As she has measured to others the likeness of Christ, so shall it be measured to her. With divine bounty there will be granted to her mind a deep knowledge of Christ, to her heart a great love of Christ, and to her life a sublime sense of utter dedication to the Cause *she* has found in Christ.

---

[5]Luke 6:38.

2

The New Excellence

An Address Delivered at the National Catholic Educational Association, International Amphitheatre, Chicago, Illinois, April 22, 1960

From the very foundation and formulation of the Catholic faith, women have been ready for whatever excellence was asked of them. When that "excellence" was ministering to Christ and His disciples as they walked the hills and plains of Judea instructing the ignorant, counseling the doubtful, healing the sick, they measured up to the demand. When "excellence" called for their loyal presence as consolers among the rabble that prodded Christ to Calvary, they were there and persevered at the foot of the Cross. When "excellence" in formulating post-resurrection doctrine was required, women, represented by Mary, were in the Cenacle among the apostles newly touched by the Paraclete with Tongues of fire and truth.

Down the centuries women, as a part of the Church, pursued excellence from the time of Peter I to John XXIII. This is doubly and undeniably true of religious women since the inception of cloistered and active Orders. This statement needs no documentation, it is part of our history and of our heritage, and notably so in the new world.

What was the excellence demanded of religious women when they first came to America as missionaries or as members of American-founded Communities? It was that *excellence* insisted upon by Bishops when they told their priests: "First build your parish schools, otherwise you will never need a parish church." Amid the alien hostilities of a new land with new immigrants

13

in search of new freedoms, it was the deepening and solidifying of the faith, making it safe amid the bigotry and the prejudices of Puritans. Excellence then, was teaching religion as the first and fundamentally important R of those that were to accompany it in the little red schoolhouses or parish halls where reading, writing and arithmetic were urged as the beginning of the American school system of education.

That excellence as emphasized in these goals has long since been proved by the long, difficult, heart-breaking but finally successful ascent to leadership of American Catholics today. Sisters have lived through, and have come a long way from the days of Maria Monk, *The Menace,* and the other would-be deterrents to Catholic excellence that dogged our steps from the very day the *Mayflower* sailed into Cape Cod Bay.

God alone knows the stouthearted determination, the will-to-excellence that animated the religious teachers of the post-colonial era of American history of education. They passed—not smoothly, but with pain and hardship and undaunted courage—to another type of excellence when Sisters' *Academies for Young Ladies* were established. These academies earned an enviable reputation for culture, and each institution boasted of at least two or three teachers of intellectual distinction whose influence permeated and gave substance to curricula that mocks the snap courses and easy-way-to-learning marked by the later influence of Dewey and the Progressivists. We may smile indulgently at courses labeled "Logic for Young Ladies," but we cannot deny the solidity of the grammar, composition, rhetoric and mathematics that turned out students who could read, write, and spell correctly, as well as concentrate on algebra and geometry.

Later, when men like Eliot of Harvard urged the elective system upon us as an excellence we could ill afford to miss, we followed secular schools into Dewey-designed curricula that made self-expression and "life-adjustment" far more important than solid academic foundations. We saw then the confusing of excellence with pragmatism, where able students elected soft courses and neglected subject matter that required rigorous application. To the student's way of thinking a course that "will help me make a living" was far more vital than a course that "will help me how to live." Softer curricula paved the way for mass education, or emphasis on mass education seemed to make the softer curricula necessary. In it all a kind of excellence was pursued, the quantitative excellence of providing something for everybody, since everybody was seeking education at the secondary level, which was but a prelude to making college necessary—or wanted—by everybody.

The sine qua non of excellence was the acceptance of our schools by a regional accrediting agency, and the agencies insisted that the type of education given be suited to the type of student entering our schools. The "type" has always been the same—the average, the below-or-above average, and the gifted. In our need to conform to the mode of the day—and the requirements of accrediting agencies (which demanded something for everybody)—we all but glorified vocational education because it so easily answered the most frequent question of our students: "What good will this course do me?"

No one can ever accuse our teaching Sisters of falling behind the Joneses in the matter of keeping our schools up-to-date with commerce, cooking, and shop courses, though the up-to-dateness, in the end, told on our goals of excellence.

In it all a definite pattern can be seen. Sisters, good strategists that they are, always manage to deliver the goods demanded of them. In an earlier century when the idea of excellence dictated an almost overemphasis on religion, the Sisters turned out stout defenders of the faith, indeed, under the leadership of the clergy they turned out the Body Faithful. When, in the interests of a more advanced Catholic education, it became clear that logic was a necessary adjunct to the Christian culture of young women, the Sisters produced solid courses in logic. When vocational education became the rage in the 1930s and a depression-minded and pragmatic people called for "useful courses," the product of our Catholic schools won prizes in homemaking and woodwork. Because America honors first and foremost the common man—in the blue shirt sleeves or white collar—the schools outdid one another in producing the common man, plain, practical, and full of common sense, the man who was on his way with a dime toward making his first million. In the quest for this excellence, the Sisters were not found wanting.

Now why do I seem to emphasize the Sisters as accomplishing these excellences? Let me hasten to admit that the 11,000 priests and the 4,000 teaching Brothers have indeed helped to make our country what it is today. But the nearly one hundred thousand teaching Sisters in the United States have the heavier burden of responsibility, for they are, one might say, in possession of the unfolding, developing Catholic mind from kindergarten through college. There are to be sure a few boys who escape to segregated Catholic schools at the upper grade and the secondary level, but relatively speaking, not too many. In the overall view of Catholic school education the Sisters hold Catholic minds a captive audience at least through high school.

This means, then, that Sisters lay the groundwork for the intellectual, social, and spiritual growth of the Catholic school population. In our grade schools it is Sister who first leads the budding mind into the intricacies of word-recognition and vocabulary building; it is Sister who first introduces the child to the wonderful world of books and develops a love (or a hatred) of reading; it is Sister who opens the wonderful door of knowledge and inspires (or destroys) a love of learning; it is Sister who continues to enkindle (or kill) a curiosity about the universe.

"All that I am, or ever hope to be—intellectually—I owe to Sister! Long before the time I reach Father Smith or Professor Jones or Brother John I have learned to love or to hate school. I look upon the boy or girl who studies hard as a sage or a fool. I have made my decision as to whether I wish to be a 'plain common man' (with a growing bank account) or a scholar of distinction."

This may be a holy and a wholesome thought, it can also be terrifying. For it means that many of the academic and intel-

lectual ills of the day—as well as the glory of accomplishment—
can be chalked up to our Sisters who have played so large and
strategic a part in the pursuit of excellence in the Catholic school
system. In a word, it means that Sisters have a great share in the
educational status quo today.

Now what is the status quo?

Long before the advent of Sputnik and Lunik, Catholic educators were viewing with alarm the lack of intellectual creative-
ness among Catholic scholars. In fact, voices were raised to ask
where ARE Catholic scholars. Perhaps the most accusing and
at the same time the most influential voices are those of Bishop
Wright and of Monsignor Tracy Ellis, who still protest that
we Catholics, religious and laity alike, are not answering the
call to the vocation of the intellectual life. For just as truly as
in the early days of the Church we had the call to spread and
develop the faith, so today we have a further call first to use our
own intellectual gifts to their full capacity, and then develop
those of our students to their fullest potential—all for the honor
and glory of God.

Now, isn't it true, Sisters, that if this essay were making an
appeal for missionaries, for the need to spread the faith in
backward countries, it would meet with irresistible enthusiasm?
Spreading the faith, giving firmer emphasis to excellence in the
teaching of religion, awakens a response in every dedicated heart.
If this essay made appeal for greater international understanding,
for a better expression of the brotherhood of man, it would find
strong echo in our hearts, for fraternal and unlimited charity is
an invitation we can understand and embrace with heroic abandon.

But this essay proposes that every religious teacher has a
vocation to intellectual excellence within the framework of her
potential—and it hopes to sound a clarion call to all religious
to manifest the same zeal in fostering and realizing this vocation
as religious in the early days of America sought to spread the
faith; the same zeal with which we followed secular leadership
in making our secondary schools a mecca of technical and "life-

adjustment" education. And I might add, the same zeal with which we have, until now, at least, made our colleges available to even the less than mediocre students who applied.

I well know what I ask when I plead with Sisters to recognize the call to intellectual excellence. We are all familiar with the antiintellectual climate of our country today, and of American Catholicism especially. If antiintellectual be too strong a term, let me say intellectual anemia. I assume that you agree with the formidable list of authorities who could be quoted—and who have been quoted by Monsignor Ellis in his treaties *American Catholics and the Intellectual Life*. I leave to this eminent educator and to others of his stature to deal with the problem on the national level. My not-so-modest hope is that those of us dedicated to Catholic education in our grades, high schools and colleges for women may thoughtfully examine our own personal attitude toward the intellectual life. Do we give it the same emphasis as we strive to give our spiritual life, and our social life of fraternal charity within the framework of our Community spirit?

Would not a careful appraisal admit these factors as true: To a certain degree we ambivalently fear and sneer at the intellectual. It is quite the American attitude, but as religious dedicated to the practice of humility and obedience, we excuse our attitude by leaning heavily on the dicta of certain spiritual writers, "Knowledge puffeth up." Leaning is such an easy posture, and while we observe the behest of *Christian Perfection,* "Let us not read to become learned. . . ." "Read little, meditate much," we steer away from the challenging example of Paul's brilliant intellectual labors.

From our novitiate days we have been warned against intellectual pride and certainly warning against pride in any of its forms is to be heeded. But how can we get our thinking straight if we persist in believing that to praise a Sister for getting straight A's in her university courses will contribute to her pride, but praising a Sister for baking delicious bread is an act of fraternal charity? We assent dutifully to such statements as "It is character that counts, not intellectual endowment," but intelligence prompts us to ask: can there be character without at least an average amount of intellectual endowment?

"Be good, sweet maid, and let who will be clever" is as glaring a bit of sophistry as ever a poet indulged. It takes mental acumen to be good; it takes even more to attain the goal dearest and nearest our hearts—spiritual excellence.

By our very dedication we make profession of striving after sanctity, and not one of us—though knowing the difficulty—hesitates to admit that this is her chief personal goal, her promised objective. Now unless we properly assess our call to the intellectual, upon which foundation sanctity, to be real, must rest, we shall never be moved to enter the arena of ideas with which today challenges us. And the first idea to be pondered is that excellence, perfection, sanctity are terms that can be equated. Let us be honest, Sisters, we do find it difficult to reconcile intellectualism and sanctity. It is so much easier—and safer—to quote the Cure of Ars when we speak of humility than Thomas Aquinas, yet who is to say was the lowlier in his own opinion?

The character of one's sanctity—or spiritual excellence—is determined by the times in which he lives. An overall view of the history of the Church shows that at different times a certain pattern of sanctity and a certain type of saint developed to meet the needs or the perils of the day. When love of riches and luxuries threatened clergy and laity alike, Francis Assisi came to preach the charms of poverty; during the ravages of the plague St. John of God and his Brother Hospitalers emerged to fight the Black Death; when Christians were enslaved by infidels the Order for the Redemption of Captives sprang up; when Protestantism and hydra-headed heresy assailed dogma, Ignatius of Loyola and his intrepid sons came into being to defend the Church. When the Church's need was for charity, motivated by faith, Vincent de Paul made his "synthesis of Charity" which, for more than three centuries, has been carried out by the congregations of men and women that he founded who were aided by the vast number of the laity he organized. In our own day we have witnessed the Maryknoll Order answering the need for a more marked missionary zeal. The School of Martyrs, founded on Calvary, and which prevailed for the first few centuries of the Church's existence, has always "kept" in some part of the world even unto our own day.

In all this activity excellence is sought—the spiritual excellence that must underscore all noble deeds. Whether it be the charity of Christ Crucified moving to deeds of heroic charity; whether it be the living and dying martyrdom of a Mindzenty or a Stepinac, or the daily intellectual endeavors of saving souls from false winds of doctrine and false gods of materialism—each activity is marked by its own brand of perfection so that we may say, in a sense, that the emphasis in the Catholic Church has always been on excellence, an excellence not always attained in its fullness but an excellence always attempted and pursued.

Nevertheless—something more is demanded today, something more than we are giving. We are the religious teachers through whose hands the Catholic school population passes from kindergarten through college. Are we responsible for the attitude that prevails today toward intellectual distinction, an attitude deplored by educators like Bishop Wright, Monsignor Ellis, and some of our eminent Catholic lay leaders? Have we helped to generate the contempt, or at least the disregard in which the so-called "egghead" is held? Are we to blame that so few Catholics distinguish themselves in the field of scholarship? Certainly, there has never been a time when more Catholics held high office in the state and federal government, and among the industrial millionaires of our country Catholics can stand up and be counted. But as yet we have failed to emulate Europe in producing Catholic men of distinction in the field of philosophy, science and letters. What is needed to right this wrong, to compensate for this defect?

Sisters, what we need today is what we have needed and given in every day, an allegiance to excellence, but to a *newer* excellence, an excellence that until today we have not sought, even as a by-product, but which today must be one of our goals —emphatic excellence in the intellectual arena.

How and where shall we begin? . . . Where and how do we begin to pursue spiritual excellence? Where we are, admitting our shortcomings and making a firm purpose of amendment. First I think we should admit that we ourselves have not held intellectual endeavor in high esteem, hence we were unable to pass on a right attitude toward intellectual achievement to our students. Oh, yes, we have always sought the *intellect*—we have wanted our students to use their minds, to learn to read, write, speak and perform; but we have placed emphasis on specialization: on *doing* well. We have sought *intellect* rather than the intellectual. Breathes there here any teacher who over the years has consciously and consistently said to herself, whether she teaches fourth grade, fourth year high or college seniors, *I shall concentrate on turning out at least one intellectual this year?* Or have we thought in terms of producing good readers, good writers, good scientists, good poets? True, these are parts of the whole, but we profess to be teaching the whole man.

Having acknowledged our deficiencies, having made a firm purpose of amendment, let us look around us at the newer excellence and appraise it. What is the newer excellence? In general, it may be said, a concentration on intellectual excellence, and let us add, the excellence of the whole man. We can easily err if we limit our sights to one field where newer excellences are demanded, such as in the sciences and the languages.

Each Saturday, in St. Louis, a Washington University expert in physics teaches a class of ten-year-olds advanced science. In turn, these ten-year-olds go to a center each week to conduct a class for teachers. The teachers, having learned and even specialized in science a decade ago, are presumably lacking in modern content and technique—the ten-year-olds supply them with both. The experiment is said to be most successful. Certainly it is a newer excellence when teachers are taught by ten-year-old pupils. But there is something rather fine in the approach.

It is far to the right of the day when teachers were accused of "putting down" any aggressive leadership or spontaneous questions from the mentally elite within their classes. It is a positive step toward making teachers more alert, more respectful of their students, and making the students themselves push out the frontiers of knowledge.

We might begin here. We can encourage our students to read, do research and share their findings in intellectual pursuits connected with the classroom, or even those that are done as extracurricular activities. We can give these students a *right* attitude toward intellectualism and toward intellectuals so that they will set their own sights higher and strive for intellectual excellence, and for excellence as an intellectual.

But isn't it right here that we meet a stumbling block? Don't we doubt, in a way, that there can be excellence as an intellectual? Four or five hundred years before Christ, Socrates told the world that an intellectual—a philosopher—would always be accused of having his head in the clouds, a much-used phrase in our own day to derogate the learned man. How many times have we said, "But intellectuals are so impractical! They never have their feet on the ground. They're all theory." Even if it were true (and I concede that it happens, but is not a necessary adjunct of intellectualism), couldn't we spare a few Catholics to the reflective life? Must we needle them, must we malign them? Can we not conceive of one man to produce ideas and of another to put them in practice?

But intellectuals need not be impractical. And perhaps they would not be, nor would they withdraw to an ivory tower to speculate, or to an academic island to evolve theories if they were made to feel more welcome, more understood by their fellowman. Isn't it a fact that we are inherently suspicious of the person who has a love of scholarship for its own sake? We mistrust his dedication to an intellectual apostolate as something that will lead inevitably to intellectual pride and to coldness in the works of charity. Here is where our spiritual reading prompts us to remember that it will avail but little to discourse profoundly if we have not humility. But has it been definitely proved that a man who discourses profoundly cannot be humble, or that a man who can define contrition cannot, at the same time, feel contrition?

Probably, among religious, nothing has impeded intellectual excellence more than the faulty reasoning that because moral excellence is the first pursuit in our schools, the intellectual virtues must be soft-pedaled; that in our own lives, since the moral virtues come first the intellectual virtues must perforce come last, and preferably in no outstanding manner, lest the proud be sent empty away. I predict that, in America, it will be a long time before we unlearn the faulty reasoning of equating pride with intellectual excellence.

We have said that the religious have always been ready for the needs of the day. What is the chief need we have today, of all times? Is it not to fight the isms and the ideologies of a world that is crassly materialistic? What is the national scene for which we are preparing students to take their place as both leaders and followers? It is a scene that faces international intrigue and possible violence on all sides, but the violence and the intrigue are based on ideas that we must fight to hold our own place in a world that has gone intellectual whether we wish to acknowledge that fact or not. Khrushchev might have been a peasant, risen from the ranks, a worker, a man of the people, but he rose to first place by reason of his brain, and we are afraid of his ideas, his theories—not because they are moral or immoral but because of his extreme intellectual dedication to these ideas.

Doctrines have always been more frightening than deeds precisely because they are intellectual, and not, like deeds, concrete, something that you can touch, and harm, and destroy. Indeed, it was our Lord's doctrine rather than His deeds that brought Him to death. We might even say it was because He insisted upon being an intellectual that He was crucified. He stirred up hatred by His doctrine of love, and disciple-ship and Son-ship with God. One doctrine was especially disturbing. "Unless ye eat My flesh and drink My blood. . . ." The crowds found it a hard saying, we are told, and walked no more with Him. Had He not insisted and insisted upon one important idea, "I am Christ, the Son of the Living God," He would have been allowed to go His way doing good among the people. They admired His deeds, they loved His miracles. But He stirred them up with new ideas. He had to die.

Right here we might pause to ask if one of the reasons for too few following Christ in the world of ideas is the fear of suffering and of misinterpretation? Are we afraid to give our intellectual powers full play lest our companions misunderstand—and walk no more with us? Or will we be branded as eggheads? Many a stout heart, ready for martyrdom, has quailed before ridicule. Yet I think it is neither of these two things. It has already been said and history proves it, Sisters have an amazing amount of fortitude. Once they know they are right they are not afraid to proceed in the face of death. It is something else, I think: By our religious vocation we are called to a communal life, and deeply ingrained in us is a suspicion, a distrust of exclusiveness, a prime adjective hurled at intellectuals. They are inclined to be exclusive; in a sense, they are deviates. It follows, then, that since the intellectual so often seeks fulfillment in aloofness from his brethren, we will have little of him, or, I should say, of her. Since the intellectual usually yields to the innate instinct of the reflective mind to walk alone (witness the hermits of old), in Community such a one is regarded as a variant. We find it difficult indeed to square the ways of a deviate, a variant, with the communal excellences of the religious life.

This was once true, but, Sisters, it need not always be true, and this is the heart of the matter. *Now* is a different time from *then*. Today the Holy See is urging all of us to serve the cause of Jesus Christ and of His Church in the way that the world demands *today,* and the state of the world today demands that we defend Christian ideas, Christian thought, on every level. Fire must be fought with fire, and we are at war with isms and ideologies. We need intellectual power as never before, but we are not asked to develop intellectual excellence in isolationism.

This is a crusade, Sisters, as true a crusade as Peter the Hermit ever preached. In that first crusade no knight was asked to go off alone; rather he was asked to join his excellence to that of his fellow-knights. In this crusade you are asked to throw your javelin into delivering the holy land of education, to free it from the bondage of mediocrity, the tyranny of overconformity, the infidelity of a too facile followership.

Now is the acceptable time, the day of intellectual renaissance. Never before in the history of the Church has the Holy See been so concerned with the spiritual, the intellectual and the professional preparation of Sisters for the Church's apostolate. At Rome, in the very shadow of the Vatican is Regina Mundi, a Pontifical Institute established for Higher Theology of Sisters. Not for Sisters and lay women, for Sisters only. From the Sacred Congregation of Religious come directives, repeated and urgent directives for the establishment of Juniorates where young religious will find no dichotomy in the spiritual and intellectual life. This is giving young religious an excellent start—or rather let me say it is giving young religious a start in excellence. But when these young recruits join our ranks they must find in us veterans that same educational integrity, that high regard of learning for learning's sake, that degree of spiritual and intellectual scholarship they have come to associate with the religious life—and in us they must find it in a greater degree.

Today is a new day in a new world where intellectual excellence must be our normal atmosphere, not an emergency inhalation of mental oxygen. There was a day—an older day—when rightfully we gave first place to the spread of faith and devotional practice. Later, we added the cultural influence of our select schools and academies with solid curricula to suit the times. In the thirties we certainly went all out for the frills and fancies of American mass education with its emphasis on something for everybody. But today calls for today's excellence—an intellectual approach more dedicated and embracing than any we made in the past, an excellence in personal scholarship that will manifest itself in a newer type of curricula.

For example, there is a specific excellence that we can emphasize today, and I think it can well be called a *newer* excellence. It is that heretofore we gave short shrift to world history and almost nothing to world literature at the undergratuate level. We have seemed to take it as an axiom that our students should know their own world and never mind the neighbor. Today this cannot be. Transportation has annihilated distance, and the Far East is coming nearer and the Near East is coming closer and we are but half-educated men if we know only the history and ideologies, literature and fine arts of the Western world and know none of these things about our Eastern brother. The idea might well be advanced that had America known more of the ideals and dreams expressed in the literature, art and music of the Asians, the Africans, of the whole Eastern world, America would have distinguished herself in world affairs with greater understanding and sympathy. Her donations of money would have bought more in the way of goodwill and brotherly love than the American dollar has been able to buy when given by ambassadors who did not take the trouble to know even the language of the countries in which their embassies were located.

This is meant as no diatribe against *The Ugly American;* it asserts only that we have woefully underestimated the power of language and overestimated the power of the dollar to help us put across our ideas and ideals. We have been helplessly unaware of the ideologies, the customs, the mores and the meanings in civilizations that are not our own. It is one of the newer excellences of our day that is repairing this evil by a new emphasis on World Cultures as one of our more important undergraduate courses today. We religious Sisters cannot afford to be left out of this movement, for we, perhaps more than our lay colleagues, realize the importance and the need to understand our brother, to take a global view of the world's needs and claims upon us; for in the first analysis we may well measure ourselves by the golden rule of understanding our brother, even as we may in the final analysis be judged on how well we have loved him.

The crusade of which I speak, however, does more than invite you to become a better teacher, giving students a clearer notion of what their attitude toward learning should be. It calls you, personally, to hearken to the invitation to become an intellectual, a leader, a strategist in the world of ideas and of understanding because the times CALL for this.

How can we answer this call to a crusade for personal intellectual activity? Among many there are three things that we can do: (1) We can enroll in a summer session somewhere and take one or two courses in a strictly intellectual field—history, literature or a language. Perhaps we ought to promise ourselves that we'll attend a summer session (and study intensively) at least every other year. (2) During the school term we can organize as a faculty group to study the Great Books. I can testify personally to the rich stimuli such an activity offers. (3) We might induce a theologian to address the faculty of our school once a month to bring us up-to-date on the newest advances in this all-important field. All three of these ideas imply correlated reading in the subject matter of our choice—a wide reading that will engender ideas and provoke serious discussion.

Somewhere I read a warning that this emphasis on a newer excellence is but a call to greater and grander courses in science. Let us not go overboard in this area, Sisters. Science is and always will be of great importance; but you and I are called to instruct others unto justice, the justice of the full man, the total man. Our vocation is not to beep nor merely to interpret the beeps of Sputnik in orbit. Our reward will be not to go round and round in circles like satellites, but to shine as the stars in the firmament. Man is still the proper study of mankind, and the humanities, which include languages, best help to this understanding, especially if the humanities are built up and integrated on a firm base of philosophy and theology. Let us, at least, give the humanities equal emphasis with science.

As has been reiterated in this essay, Sisters have always been ready for whatever demands have been made upon them. Today's demands are new and different. The Holy See has sounded a call to intellectual excellence. We cannot all be geniuses or artisans, any more than we can all be wise men; but we can and shall drink as deeply from the springs of wisdom as our potential will allow. We can do this, Sisters, for by reason of the grace of God, our ethnic origins and our Catholic Faith, we are the heirs of all the intellectual ages. When the waters of baptism changed our pagan progenitors to Christians our Gaelic and Gothic genes lost none of their virility. The song of the Druid chanters has changed, but the singers live on.

"With a fulcrum and a lever, give me room and I can move the world," said Archimedes. For us, the sacred commission to learn and to teach is our fulcrum; the strong enduring love of Christ is our lever. Come, Sisters. Let us move the world!

3

Four Stories of Flannery O'Connor

It comes as good news that Flannery O'Connor is at work on a new collection of short stories. She has already completed "Greenleaf,"[1] "A View of the Woods," "The Enduring Chill," "The Comforts of Home," and "The Partridge Festival."

Critics of this second volume of stories will probably be more discerning than were those of her two novels and the ten distinctive stories published in 1955 under the title *A Good Man Is Hard to Find*. It is to be hoped so, at least, since perceptive reviews and penetrating analyses of her stories will insure a more discriminating enjoyment of her writings.

Admittedly, Miss O'Connor is not easy reading unless one is satisfied with the casual, horror-story approach. Then one may dismiss her as "gratuitously grotesque" and "brutally ironic," as several of her reviewers have done. But the more thoughtful reader will recognize that the knowledge, the artistry, the vivid clarity and intense vitality with which Miss O'Connor writes of a people and a locale she knows and obviously loves are not brought into play merely to exploit horror and portray violence. Rather, the perceptive reader soon discerns that Flannery O'Connor uses her brilliant gifts for a specific purpose based on a particular plan.

This purpose Miss O'Connor makes uncompromisingly clear when she speaks of her view of reality:

---

[1]"Greenleaf" has been reviewed elsewhere as the 1957 O. Henry prize winner.

I see from the standpoint of Christian orthodoxy. This means that for me the meaning of life is centered in our Redemption by Christ and that what I see in the world I see in its relation to that. I don't think that this is a position that can be taken half way or one that is particularly easy in these times to make transparent in fiction.[2]

Cavil with this statement as we may, a purpose is so intrinsically subjective that one cannot reject an author's claim without impugning his integrity and sincerity. To those who do reject this claim on the grounds that Miss O'Connor seeks only to shock by presenting the grotesque, she answers:

The novelist with Christian concerns will find in modern life distortions which are repugnant to him, and his problem will be to make these appear as distortions to an audience which is used to seeing them as natural; and he may well be forced to take ever more violent means to get his vision across to this hostile audience. When you can assume that your audience holds the same beliefs as you do, you can relax a little and use more normal ways of talking to it; when you have to assume that it does not, then you have to make your vision apparent by shock—to the hard of hearing you shout, and for the almost blind you draw large and startling figures.[3]

Miss O'Connor makes three points: (1) She sees all reality in relation to redemptive grace and can never take a halfway position in this view. (2) In order to have her vision of reality understood she often feels obliged to use violent means. (3) She finds it difficult to make this purpose transparent in fiction today.

Miss O'Connor further develops her purpose:

---

[2]Flannery O'Connor, "The Fiction Writer and His Country," Granville Hicks, ed., *The Living Novel,* a Symposium (New York: Macmillan, 1957), p. 162.

[3]*Ibid.,* p. 163.

My own feeling is that writers who see by the light of their Christian faith will have, in these times, the sharpest eyes for the grotesque, for the perverse, and for the unacceptable. . . . The reason for this attention to the perverse is the difference between their beliefs and the beliefs of their audience. Redemption is meaningless unless there is cause for it in the actual life we live, and for the last few centuries there has been operating in our culture the secular belief that there is no such cause.[4]

Such is Miss O'Connor's uncompromising statement of an uncompromising purpose. This purpose, she admits, is difficult to make transparent in her stories. It certainly is not immediately evident to the ordinary reader and, I would say, is never obvious even to the perceptive reader; but no one can read far in Flannery O'Connor's writings without becoming aware of a certain pattern running through her novels and stories. This awareness of a pattern, unclear and elusive at first, returns with insistent demand for identity, an identity that will not be denied yet which at first defies recognition. One cannot dismiss it with an appreciative murmur: "Oh, this reminds me of Bloy . . . that, of Mauriac. . . ." Some of the characters and incidents in her stories may well recall characters and incidents in Bloy and Mauriac but Miss O'Connor reminds one only of Miss O'Connor.

Of the plan underlying her stories, Miss O'Connor writes in answer to those who complain that literature today is lacking in a sense of spiritual purpose and in the joy of life:

The only conscience I have to examine in this matter is my own, and when I look at stories I have written I find they are, for the most part, about people who are poor, who are afflicted in both mind and body, who have little—or at best

---

[4]*Ibid.*, p. 162.

a distorted—sense of spiritual purpose, and whose actions do not apparently give the reader a great assurance of the joy of life.[5]

The clue to understanding Miss O'Connor's stories lies in recognizing the relation of her purpose to her plan: She will show the mystery of redemptive grace at work in everyday life. Her base of operation will be among poor and deprived people whose spiritual perception is at best distorted and without joy. If, to this stated purpose and plan we add our own insights as to a pattern, the haunting, yet elusive quality in Miss O'Connor's writings stands identified: universal experience such as one is confronted with in the Holy Scriptures. Consciously or unconsciously there emanates the influence, not so much of Bloy, nor of Mauriac, nor of Graham Greene, but of the Bible with its preoccupation with Redemption foretold and Redemption achieved.

It will be interesting to observe whether this pattern of influence, substantial, but always subtle, will be as noticeable in later stories as it was in most of the first collection and is in four of the latest. One reads with quickened insight if one keeps these factors—purpose, plan and pattern—in mind. "The Partridge Festival," appearing in *The Critic,* February, 1961, is, I believe, the first of Miss O'Connor's works to appear in a Catholic periodical. Here we identify that haunting sense of universal experience—truth—and through recognition of it, we penetrate the purpose, plan and pattern of the story.

The setting for "The Partridge Festival" is a small, inconsequential, off-the-beat southern town named Partridge. It is also the world. With its Azalea Festival and Miss Partridge Azalea, it is Atlantic City with its beauty contests and Miss America. It is Washington, D.C., with its Cherry Tree Festival and Miss Cherry Blossom. It is Houston, Texas, with its Cotton Carnival and Queen Cotton. It is London. It is Tokyo. It is New Delhi. For that matter it is the Garden of Eden, had the primal couple, after

---

[5]*Ibid.,* p. 161.

their Fall, been permitted to remain there: Eve's sorrows multiplying with her conceptions, and Adam tilling the ground in the sweat of his brow.

The citizens of Partridge are the stock-in-trade of the human race. If they strike the reader as bizarre, out of proportion, overly emphasized, it is because Miss O'Connor detaches them from the world climate that begot them, and focuses the attention of the reader on each individually. This has the same effect as is accomplished by inviting a person to look at an object under a powerful microscope. The viewer draws back affrighted at the sight of some horrible monster, or in disgust from some huge, misshaped, moving mass. Then he learns that the "monster" is but a tiny ant, of which there are thousands on his lawn; or the loathsome "mass" is but a speck of scum from a pool in his back yard. Partridge is a microcosm, as like the universe as is the miniature globe on a schoolboy's desk; like the huge globe in a national planetarium.

Partridge sells beauty. Through a well-ballyhooed, tradition-tagged annual azalea festival, it turns the lovely, heady, indigenous plant into a blatantly proclaimed "Money Crop." In this, Partridge conforms to the universal pattern, for beauty is sold everywhere. Railroads sell it in their "scenic routes"; movies and TV in face and figure; realtors in their "palm-and-pine" slogans; hotels with their "ocean views"; Partridge with its azaleas. Here then, in this cosmic setting, Miss O'Connor raises the curtain and permits plot, characters, and incidents to unfold.

Enter sin in its simplest, elemental form: greed, avarice, revenge, murder. Partridge's wealthy, repulsive miser, a man named Singleton, refuses to pay the price of a festival badge. For this lack of patriotic spirit he is shamelessly roughhoused by his fellow citizens. In revenge, he shoots six of them dead. Judged insane, he is committed to the state institution at Quincy.

Enter self-deification. This sin, more complex and vastly more of the devil than the crime of murder, is incarnate in Calhoun, the twenty-three-year-old great-grandnephew of one of the founders of Partridge. Calhoun, in emancipating himself from Partridge, emancipated himself also from every vestige of the Christian Faith in which he has been reared. Ostensibly, he returns to his native city to attend the Azalea Fair. His real intention is to write a novel of the mass murder, wherein the town of Partridge would be shamed and Singleton glorified as a man who fought for his personal freedom, who refused to run with the herd.

Calhoun has a deeper, more obscure, near-psychotic motive. He is a sort of sane schizophrenic who, for three months of the year is, to his profound shame and disgust, a successful salesman of refrigerators, airconditioners and boats. During the other nine months he strives to live up to what he deems is his real self: "a rebel-artist-mystic." Without an ounce of talent for writing, he is, against his will, phenomenally successful as a salesman.

> In the face of a customer, he was carried outside himself, his face began to beam and sweat, and all of his complexities left him; he was in the grip of a drive as strong as the drive of some men for liquor. . . . He was so good at it that the Company had given him an achievement scroll.

His novel on Singleton will, he hopes, free him from guilt feelings connected with his original innocence as demonstrated in his skill as a salesman.

Enter an ally. Since "male and female made He them," Calhoun finds an unexpected ally in a young neighbor, Mary Elizabeth, also a native of Partridge. Instinctively they dislike each other but Calhoun sees that her contempt for the town and its people surpasses even his own. She, too, has cast off the trammels of Christian belief. She, too, would write a masterpiece holding Partridge up to scorn and Singleton to veneration. In her "non-fiction study" Singleton would be made a "Christ figure"— a myth, of course, she assures Calhoun, since she is an atheist, but Singleton could be shown as a symbol of expiation, representing that in the town of Partridge it was expedient that one man should die.

Calhoun is quick to identify Singleton with Christ as the details of the murder unfold during his interviews with a cross section of the town's inhabitants: Singleton had a mock trial—as did Christ before Pilate. Singleton was shamefully beaten and bound; Jesus was mocked and scourged and spat upon. Singleton was imprisoned with a goat "guilty of the same offense" (not buying a badge); Christ was crucified between two thieves.

Along with the details of Singleton's sufferings, Calhoun turns up many of the traits with which the town of Partridge—and the world—abounds: cruelty, vicious calumny, hatreds, grudges and greed are the social life-stream. Fitting the pieces together to suit his theory, Calhoun bitterly declaims: "Singleton was only the instrument. Partridge itself is guilty . . . Singleton's the scape-goat. He's laden with the sins of the community. Sacrificed for the guilt of others." In identifying Singleton with Christ, Calhoun reveals how completely he himself identifies with Singleton.

"He was an individualist," Calhoun said. "A man who would not allow himself to be pressed into a mold of his inferiors. A non-conformist. He was a man of depth living among caricatures and they finally drove him mad and unleashed all his violence on themselves."

So completely has the Christ-Calhoun-Singleton image merged in the boy's mind that a rude shock awaits him at the Quincy State Institution where he goes—at Mary Elizabeth's baiting—to meet Singleton face to face. He foresees that the encounter, painful as it will be to see the man's sufferings, will rouse him from his commercial instincts; once and for all it will somehow prove that every man is created equally an artist. Thus will he rise above his despised single talent of salesmanship to become what he most desires, the rebel-artist-mystic. For Mary Elizabeth it is much the same. She, too, has come to see in Singleton a self-image of whom she would coolly write with detached "humani-tarianism": she will present him as a hero, the "historical Christ" for whom the small-town rabble had decreed persecution and death.

Thus psychologically prepared to see Singleton, they wait in
the shabby visitor's room with its barred windows and "a peculiar
odor that met them at once like an invisible official."

There seemed an intense stillness about them although the
place was anything but quiet. . . . Closer at hand a steady
monotonous cursing broke the silence with machine-like reg-
ularity. . . . The two sat together as if waiting for something
portentous. . . .

Each has a sudden impulse to run but it is too late. Heavy foot-
steps pounding closer fail to drown out the machine-like crack-
ling of curses as the door opens.

Singleton, refusing to walk, is dragged in by two burly at-
tendants. Clothed only in a hospital gown and black derby hat,
he shrills amid an explosion of blasphemy: "Whadaya want with
me?" Calhoun is too stupefied to answer. Mary Elizabeth, in a
barely audible voice says, "We came to say we understand." At the
sound of a woman's voice "the old man's glare shifted to the girl
and for one instant his eyes remained absolutely still like those of
a tree-toad that had sighted his prey." There, before the shocked
and unbelieving eyes of the boy and girl, Singleton stands revealed
for what he was, for what the people of Partridge said he was, a
crafty, lecherous roué from whose spirochete-infested brain all
decent reactions had been driven, leaving only the primal, earthy
drive.

Enter salvation. With the terror and haste of Adam and
Eve fleeing the wrath of God, Calhoun and Mary Elizabeth flee
the institution. They have stood face to face with guilt, and guilt
there cannot be if there be no God. They sit in the car silently
looking at each other, in the girl's ear Singleton's lewd plea still
ringing: "Look girl . . . you and me are two of a kind. We ain't
in their class." In Calhoun there is only anguished surrender as
he accepts the miniature reflection of himself in the girl's spec-
tacles. At last they see themselves for what they are and the
shards of their disbelief fall about them, like the clay image of

themselves which they had worshipped. In the implacable reality of the true Singleton, they see the frustrating unreality of their own pseudo-selves. Christ, whom they had sought to reject, is back in possession of the temple. They stare at each other and the staring is as painful and as cleansing as a burning coal. In its purifying pain they accept themselves as their Creator has made them. Calhoun, and by association, Mary Elizabeth, sees that he will find salvation only in the honest sweat and exercise of his God-given talent; for the "Trade until I come" of the New Testament is the command for the holder of ten talents as well as for the holder of one.

In the fall of 1960, *The Kenyon Review* published "The Comforts of Home." In the opening paragraph the reader is made aware of Miss O'Connor's deftness and dexterity in delineating character as she presents the three main persons of the story. Not only are they introduced, but with an almost miraculous parsimony of words they are analyzed and their relationships one to the other made apparent. Here is Thomas' mother, the do-gooder with such burning zeal to save the sinner that she carries her benevolent intentions to the point of idiocy. With her is the utterly amoral girl, referred to by Thomas as "the slut," to whom she offers a home in a more than quixotic effort to help her. And here is the thirty-five-year-old son, Thomas, with neither his mother's drive to good nor the girl's drive to evil. Thomas is a dedicated lethargist whose God is the *Status Quo*, whose profession of faith is DON'T DISTURB. He has already found his heaven in the "comforts of home"—anything that would disturb or deprive him of these he sees as hell.

As the story, centered on the horrid problem of these three persons living under one roof, develops, the reader realizes with almost panic resentment against his own reaction, that he feels neither sympathy for the plight in which Thomas has been placed nor admiration for his efforts to repel the advances of the girl. These advances are as much a part of her nature as are the foul fumes arising from a clogged sewer. She is morally incompetent and toward her one feels a judicious, legal sternness: for society's sake and for her own she should be physically confined to an institution where she may possibly be reeducated to some degree of moral rehabilitation. Toward the mother one has a healthy feeling of anger and contempt at her cross-purpose crusading zeal.

But for Thomas! One can scarcely curb the inexorable, steadily rising disgust that mounts to the point of nausea and threatens to overflow. The reader—as well as his mother—can count on his attachment to his electric blanket, on the well-regulated house his mother manages, on the excellent meals she serves—to keep Thomas from taking any overt action that will interfere with his comfort. He can deliver ultimatums, accusing his mother of "caring nothing about his peace and comfort and working conditions," but he cannot make them good—not when they would take him away from all that his electric blanket and Morris chair imply.

And so we have a well-contrived plot, and a superb but subtle exposition of character and situation built upon those enigmatic words of the Apocalypse: "Would that you were hot or cold but because you are lukewarm I will begin to vomit you out of my mouth." The mother, with her blind, intemperate determination to help everyone in sight, is indeed "hot" and, with the best intentions in the world, as the author points out, "pursues goodness with such mindless intensity that everyone involved is made a fool of and virtue itself becomes ridiculous." Our Lord nowhere holds this up as admirable and worthy of imitation, but He does state succinctly that the hot and cold are less disgusting than the lukewarm.

The "slut" symbolizes the other extreme, the "cold." She is a human being as impervious to moral values as is a stone to water. Thomas analyzes her correctly:

He needed nothing to tell him that he was in the presence of the very stuff of corruption, but of blameless corruption because there was no responsible faculty behind it. He was looking at the most unendurable form of innocence. Absently he asked himself what the attitude of God was to this, meaning if possible to adopt it.

What God thinks has been expressed by God in the uncompromising language of Divinity, "Would that *you*, Thomas, were as hot as your mother or as cold as the slut. . . ." But Thomas once soliloquizes about his mother's pursuit of good: "Had she been in any degree intellectual, he could have proven to her from early Christian history, that no excess of virtue is justified; that a moderation of good produces likewise a moderation in evil." And thus he equates moderation with stagnation.

This is the crux of the story. In contrast to his mother with her sorrowing zeal for the whole world, and to the slut as the "most unendurable form of innocence" Thomas, outraged only when his personal comfort is threatened, stands revealed as the most loathsome form of inert guilt. Even at the close of the story when Thomas thinks he is shooting the girl, he hears the blast of his gun "as a sound that would shatter the laughter of sluts . . . and nothing be left to disturb the peace of perfect order."

Some readers of "The Comforts of Home" will see in the story's ending only a tragic miscarriage of justice. Such readers would seem to have a habitually secular outlook on life—an outlook that views the affairs of men without thought of the designs of God in them. They constitute, then, that "hostile audience" for whom Miss O'Connor claims she must use violence to interpret her meaning; they are the hard of hearing for whom she must shout; they are the near-blind for whom she must draw large and startling figures. They are the people who can behold an airplane crash and never think to remember that "not a sparrow falls without the knowledge of a compassionate Father."

The secular sees what happens to man, but with no reference to God's plans, nor to the supernatural elements that flow from them: suffering, expiation, regeneration, redemption. The practical Christian, as distinguished from the academic, will find that the finale of this story allows for and implies the action of redemptive grace working for and in three chief characters: eternal peace for the poor, bungling, well-meaning mother; salvation by way of protection for the congenitally deprived "slut"; redemption through projected suffering for Thomas, the ease-enslaved son, who will never again know the comforts of home.

"The Enduring Chill" published in *Harper's Bazaar,* July, 1958, is, in the opinion of this writer, the easiest to read of all Miss O'Connor's stories. This is not entirely a compliment because Miss O'Connor is at her best when one has to plumb the depths to discover her meaning.

There is another concern about "The Enduring Chill" that breeds a question: Is Flannery O'Connor beginning to repeat herself? So gifted a writer can afford to repeat her theme. Surely the number of ways in which one may see redemptive grace at work in the souls of men is legion and Miss O'Connor is adept and adroit at handling similarity with variety. The persistence of certain dominant ideas through the work of an author is not unusual. They are the pattern of moral experiences in youth through sharp observation and confirmed in maturity. It is in expressing these ideas that an author learns and develops his art to its most subtle and profound realization. Flannery O'Connor's success in this has been due in large part to her ability to deal with mystery as mystery. The working of grace in any soul is a mysterious process, and Flanney O'Connor treats it as such. Hence, in reading her stories one often feels that as he searches hidden truth he is oppressed by the unknown and inexplicable as he comes face to face with the deep and silent, somewhat impenetrable places of man's soul. This sense of oppression by mystery is absent in "The Enduring Chill," for Miss O'Connor is more obvious in both plot and technique. It is as if one viewed a Picasso painting of the Cubistic period entitled "Winter Tree" and lo! one saw—a tree.

Young Asbury Fox is obliged, because of illness, to return from a bohemian life in New York to the small home town in

Georgia he detests. There are no ideas, no challenges in this "desert" to a would-be artist, certainly not to one who had already destroyed "two lifeless novels, a half dozen stationary plays, (some) prosy poems and (several) sketchy short stories." Asbury has come home to die but he himself suspects that his illness is not entirely unconnected with his discovery that he will never be an artist. "He had failed his god, Art, (he muses) but he had been a faithful servant and Art was sending him Death. He had seen this from the first with a kind of mystical clarity." Since he has no other god to worship and is resentful of his mother, whose domination he blames for his lack of talent, his inability to create ("Woman, why did you pinion me?"), and whom he accuses of having domesticated his imagination, he finds home intolerable and yearns for one last "meaningful experience" before he dies.

He recalls a Jesuit he met in New York at a beatnik session of angry young men where Asbury's approaching death had been discussed. Asbury, a non-believer, had admired the priest's "taciturn, superior expression" and decided now that if he could only see a Jesuit, perhaps match wits with a man of culture, he would have one last meaningful experience before he died. His mother's prejudices were overcome easily enough—she would do anything, however ridiculous, for her ailing, suffering son.

The Jesuit who arrived from a nearby parish was very different from the intellectual Asbury had met in New York.

"I'm Father Finn—from Purrgatory" he said in a hearty voice. He had a large red face, a stiff brush of gray hair and was blind in one eye, but the good eye, blue and clear was focused sharply on Asbury. There was a grease spot on his vest.

The boy's mother, at his request, reluctantly leaves the room, and Asbury is ready for a hard, tough intellectual discussion of Joyce, the myth of the dying god, and artistic expression of creativity.

Instead, the priest brushes aside Joyce, atheism, and art as so many annoying gnats and comes to grips with reality:

> "Do you have trouble with purity?" he demanded, and as Asbury paled, he went on without waiting for an answer. "We all do, but you must pray to the Holy Ghost for it. Mind, heart and body. Nothing is overcome without prayer . . ."

It is tempting to reproduce the trenchant dialogue that follows— the best of its kind in this type of short-story writing. It is difficult to choose excerpts but one quotation is prophetic:

> "How can the Holy Ghost fill your soul when it's full of trash?" the priest roared. "The Holy Ghost will not come until you see yourself as you are—a lazy, ignorant, conceited youth!" he said, pounding his fist on the little bedside table.

The boy's mother intervenes here and the priest affably departs after giving Asbury his blessing. His parting words to Mrs. Fox float back to the exhausted boy: "He's a good lad at heart but very ignorant."

Asbury, "drawn and ravaged . . . staring in front of him with large, childish, shocked eyes" is left alone with his thought. He had told the priest that the Holy Ghost was the last thing he was looking for and the priest replied: "And He may be the last thing you get."

How the Holy Ghost finally implacably descends upon Asbury, who, after all, has only undulant fever and probably will not die, is Miss O'Connor's vision of reality seen always in the light of redemptive grace working in the human soul. It is built upon the scriptural theme "I have chosen the weak and simple of this world to confound the wise and strong."

"The Enduring Chill" is important as a story. It is the first of Miss O'Connor's that can be clearly identified as Catholic. If I say that it is easier to analyze than many of her other stories, this is not in any way to deprecate its significance. As in all true works of art—and Flannery O'Connor is undeniably a brilliant artist—the moral point is implicit, built into the story in such a way as not to be easily discernible. Indeed, this story may well be hailed as a reprieve by some of her readers who have found Miss O'Connor unduly difficult, although always rewarding.

"A View of the Woods" appeared in the 1957 fall number of *Partisan Review* and in the Foley-Burnett collection of *Best American Short Stories of 1958*. It is a typical Flannery O'Connor story, faintly redolent of her earlier "The Artificial Nigger" inasmuch as both stories deal with the fascinating, real-life phenomenon of advanced old age and very early youth in close, prolonged and comradely companionship. In this instance, it is seventy-nine-year-old Mark Fortune and his nine-year-old grandchild and namesake, Mary Fortune Pitts, whom he insists on calling Mary Fortune, ignoring the Pitts as a name despised, unworthy of his clay.

The Pitts family, of which the little girl is the youngest, live in virtual bondage on the grandfather's land. He despises his daughter, her husband and the other six grandchildren, reminding them at every turn that he is master of the house and that they are beholden to him for their very livelihood.

Mr. Fortune had allowed them, ten years ago, to move onto his place and farm it. What Pitts made went to Pitts but the land belonged to Fortune and he was careful to keep the fact before them. When the well had gone dry, he had not allowed Pitts to have a deep well drilled but had insisted that they pipe their water from the spring. He did not intend to pay for a drilled well himself and he knew that if he let Pitts pay for it, whenever he had occasion to say to Pitts, "It's my land you're sitting on," Pitts would be able to say to him, "Well, it's my pump that's pumping the water you're drinking." He would not allow them to pay rent for the same reason he would not allow them to drill a well . . . and every now and then he gave the Pittses a practical lesson by selling off a lot. Nothing infuriated Pitts more than to see him sell off a piece of the property to an outsider, because Pitts wanted to buy it himself.

With an intensity of meanness and malice hard to believe, Fortune dedicates himself to two overriding ambitions: to amass money—a process which he calls progress——while making life more miserable and precarious for the Pittses, and to instill into Mary Fortune his own sentiments of contempt for her family. In the first he succeeds deplorably. In the second he fails. For though little Mary Fortune spends most of her time in her grandfather's company, and is misjudged by her mother and beaten by her father—Pitts's great and only possible revenge on old man Fortune—she resolutely but impassively refuses to obey her grandfather's urging to "stand up to Pitts."

This love-in-conflict between the old man and his granddaughter, whom he has named in his will as sole heir to his possessions, is the heart of the story. For little Mary Fortune is a physical replica of the old man and "she was like him on the inside, too. . . . Though there was seventy years' difference in their ages the spiritual distance between them was slight." This very likeness proves, in the end, their undoing. Possessing her grandfather's singular intelligence, his strong will, his push and drive, she matches his glory in being "pure Fortune" with a silent, unconquerable pride of her own in being "pure Pitts."

The blow falls when Fortune sells his fifth lot, the two-hundred-foot frontage of the house which Mary Fortune and the other children called their "play place," her mother called "the lawn," her father called his "calf pasture" and which the entire Pitts family called "the view of the woods." Sure of his influence on the child, old Mark Fortune, with little nine-year-old Mary Fortune at his side, drives to the village store to sign the deed of sale. Less than an hour later, in a clearing facing the woods, the old man and the child lie dead; the last and violent struggle of "Pure Fortune" vs. "Pure Pitts" has ended in a tie.

In plot, characters and tone, "A View of the Woods" is an outstanding story in pure Flannery O'Connor tradition. Here the author goes to the very soul, indeed to the very meaning of redemptive grace—hope. Man can live, however barrenly, without charity. Man can live, however aimlessly, without faith. But the human heart cannot live without hope, for without hope the will to live, to struggle, to somehow survive, dies out. What made the Fall a *felix culpa* and saved the whole human race from despair was that God gave man the hope of a Redeemer. Man will fight for freedom, for health, for riches only so long as hope is not lost, for hope is his central human passion— ennobling, destructive, implacable.

Hope must have a sign or symbol, spiritual or material. It was the view of the woods across from the land on which they were suffered to live that sustained the oppressed Pittses in their bondage to the tyrannical old man Fortune. As long as they could see "the view" they need not accept his dictum, "For a grown person all roads lead either to heaven or to hell." Some day the old man would die and the land that faced the woods would be theirs. To this hope the Pittses did and could cling fiercely if not lovingly.

For old Mark Fortune there was one burning hope: to make his granddaughter into his own image and likeness, leave her his entire fortune so that "when he died she could make the rest of them jump; and he didn't doubt for a minute that she would be able to do it."

For little Mary Fortune hope worked toward someday being herself "Pure Pitts" and thus accepted and loved by her family, and perhaps of help to them, even at the cost of her grandfather's favor and fortune.

The crux of the story is not in its bloody and seemingly pointless climax, but in this fact of hope, the symbol and seal of redemptive grace; here, natural and material symbols, to be sure, but the base on which grace must work to achieve even the slow beginnings of the supernatural.

Scaled down almost infinitesimally, but still distinct, Mary

Fortune's role is curiously like that of Moses in the land of the Pharaohs. Like him she sees herself favored by the oppressor of her people, given his name, made the preferred associate and promised heir. The lot of her family closely parallels that of the Israelites under the yoke of the Egyptians, fleeing at last from a bondage no longer endurable, coming finally under the guidance of Moses to the promised land—a land which he, like his little prototype, Mary Fortune, died without seeing.

There is in the conclusion of this Mosaic story a fine legal point to ponder, and that is the crucial matter of the last will and testament of old Mark Fortune. His legatee has died minutes before he himself expired, and a dead person cannot be considered in a will. Therefore the nearest of kin become the beneficiaries . . . and so Pittses inherit the land. Thus, in a sense, did little Mary Fortune lead her people out of the land of bondage. It might be added that death, in spite of its needless violence, was for her a distinctive redemptive grace. What she might have become a few years more under the devastating tutelage of old Mark Fortune is unpleasant and unnecessary to contemplate.

Flannery O'Connor has set herself a difficult goal if she intends her new collection to surpass in excellence the ten outstanding stories in *A Good Man Is Hard to Find*. The four stories studied in these pages give us reason to believe that she will achieve this goal with distinction. She has accepted writing, or rather her avowed purpose in writing, as a vocation and she does not take this vocation lightly. She will continue to see and to feel life from the vantage point of the Mystery of the Incarnation, and she will be more than ever "concerned to have her work stand on its own feet, complete, self-sufficient and impregnable in its own right."

It is never easy to estimate a contemporary author's chance to survive nor to predict that certain works will take and hold a permanent place in literature, but I would venture to say that Miss O'Connor is destined to endure as a gifted American writer precisely because she understands that as a Catholic she can never afford to be less than an artist. "Part of the complexity of the problem for the Catholic fiction writer," she says, "will be the presence of grace as it appears in nature, and what matters for the writer is that his faith not become detached from his dramatic sense and from his vision of what is." I do not think Miss O'Connor will ever permit this detachment nor will she ever limit on the natural level what she allows herself to see.

Hence we may expect further stories informed with the action of redemptive grace, which is, after all, central and basic to the human condition. This action in the creatures of her brain will never be overt or obvious any more than the assimilation of food in the human system is obvious or overt, but it will be there for us to find that Christ died for all men and the grace of redemption flows through channels both regular and irregular. Shakespeare was never more truly Christian than when he wrote: "There's a divinity that shapes our ends, rough-hew them how we will."

I believe Miss O'Connor will continue to create characters that bring strongly to mind the poor, the lowly, the afflicted, the self-righteous, the stiff-necked, the suffering, the ignorant, the contentious that followed the steps of Christ wherever He went and that are with us today. In them we shall continue to see ourselves as we are, and if we are appalled at the revealing vision maybe we will try to do something about it.

That Miss O'Connor is influenced by Holy Scripture is my own assertion, not hers. Actually, I do not know whether she reads the Bible or not, but to me she exudes its influence, an inevitable result, it would seem, of her milieu. Born and bred in the Bible Belt of the United States, she grew up among a people to whom the Bible is all religion, where believers among the educated base their conduct on its precepts, and drink in its beauty as part of their culture; where, among the poor, the lowly, the ignorant and the deprived even the least educated hug to their hearts their often fragmentary knowledge of Holy Writ. They quote or misquote the Bible to substantiate their simple virtues or to justify revolting vice. Consciously or unconsciously this influence has rubbed off on Miss O'Connor, and the artistry and brilliancy we note in the plot and characterization of her stories are not, I believe, entirely unconnected with a familiarity with the Scriptures.

The action of redemptive grace at work in the soul of man and his response to its influence; the choice of ordinary, often poor and deprived people with a defective sense of spiritual purpose as prototypes for this action of grace; and a sensitive, perhaps subconscious use of scriptural parallels of truth and experience seem to me to constitute the purpose, plan and pattern of Miss O'Connor's writings. This threefold complex is merged into a technique so subtle, so informed with variety and versatility, so perfect that few will realize it is there. But it is palpably there, sensitizing the reader to spiritual and psychological implications that underlie the myriad and diverse phenomena of human conduct. This technique is Miss O'Connor's gift—a gift she uses with ironic humor, brilliant intellect and rare compassion.

4

Sister Bertrande Meyers' Contribution to "Flannery O'Connor—A Tribute"

Flannery O'Connor was denied the biblical life of three score and ten; actually missing two score by one short year. In number, her writings matched her years in fewness. Two novels, one collection of short stories, another collection to be published posthumously make up the sum total of her contribution to the contemporary literary world. Yet, for some fourteen of her thirty-nine years, Flannery O'Connor was a figure in that world—not a predominant figure, but one whose prominence was heightened by the controversial opinions aroused by her writings. Her proven potentialities as a writer insured that she would be kept in mind; by some, hopefully, and by others, uneasily.

For Flannery O'Connor had her fans and her foes, not in equal numbers. Her admirers, I believe, far outnumbered her adversaries; at least her admirers were more articulate, although her foes, when vocal, were almost vituperatively so. To both she was a sign and a symbol just as an anchor, a flag, a cross or a caduceus is a sign. In reviewing her life and works one cannot escape the fact that Flannery was "set for a sign that shall be contradicted" and contradictions there were aplenty. But of what was she a sign? Aye, there's the rub, for neither her admirers nor her adversaries seem sure of just what her symbolism signified. Hostile critics coined such alliterative epithets as "ferocious Flannery" and accused her of deliberately cultivating the "gratuitously grotesque" in the selection of her dramatis personae. Her admirers, with definite certainty of their admiration, but somewhat unsure of just what they admired, wrote of her perceptive skill in character delineation, of her psychological insights and her ability to face stark reality and appraise it for what it was. But most of all they applauded her creative capacity to see teeming life with its inevitable tragedy in the apparently drab, commonplace, unchallenging detail of everyday life without losing an iota of her unfailing compassion for all that is human, however erring. Actually, however, both foe and friend missed the point and purpose of Flannery O'Connor's "message" until she herself supplied the key.

WAYS OF INTERPRETATION

There are two ways of interpreting an author's meaning: one is to see and understand the author—and the message he is attempting to convey—through his writings and what they reveal. The other is to interpret the writings after coming to know the author, either by personal contact or by reading what he has to say of himself. I have an idea that Flannery would have preferred the former method, for she indeed recognized the curious fact that up until mid-1957 all critics, favorable and unfavorable of Flannery O'Connor, seemed to be saying the same thing. There isn't space to go into this, but there seemed to be an uncertainty, a vagueness and, at best, a reserved appreciation of Flannery's "perceptiveness" and an acceptance of the fact that she was skilled in drawing unusual portraits of unusual characters. This came from those who favored the author. From those who did not there were all sorts of accusations about her penchant for freaks, her refusal to deal with Catholic themes or characters, and that she seemed to revel in presenting immoral situations and amoral people for no apparent moral purpose.

Even admirers of Flannery's stories seemed somehow unsure of what point she was making, and neither friend nor foe seemed able or willing to really take her stories apart and analyze them to the satisfaction of the curious, puzzled reader. Critics described the stories, retold them in other words, but somehow they seemed unable to cope with the pattern or point up the purpose.

This was frustrating to certain fan-readers, not given to writing, for they felt that, decoded and deciphered, her stories had something very real and very Catholic and very ecumenical about them—something very fundamental to faith. Actually, Flannery came to grips with the Incarnation, to the essence of religion, the fact that Christ died for all men. It helped a great deal if the reader knew his Bible.

Then, almost as if constrained to do so, Flannery spoke up for herself. In her chapter "The Fiction Writer and His Country," a contribution to Granville Hicks' symposium *The Living Novel* (published by Macmillan in 1957), Flannery clearly states the purpose of her writing. In seven pages of unassailable logic and uncompromising phrases, written in her own cogent style, with its seasoned sarcasm, biting irony, and saving humor, Flannery brings into sharp focus the import of her fiction: "I am no disbeliever in spiritual purpose," she says, "and I am no vague believer. I see from the standpoint of Christian orthodoxy. This means for me the meaning of life is centered in our Redemption by Christ and that what I see in the world I see in its relation to that." She added, not as an afterthought, but out of her experience of being so often misinterpreted, "I don't think that this is a position that can be taken halfway or one that is particularly easy in these times to make transparent in fiction."

WRITING IS A VOCATION

For her friends and for all who wrote fairly of her, this statement was taken at face value and used as a sort of Rosetta stone after 1957. A spate of articles followed with titles to prove this acceptance and to disprove her earlier critics: "Flannery O'Connor and the Reality of Sin" (*Catholic World,* January 1959), "Flannery O'Connor's Way: Shock with Moral Intent" (*Renascence,* Summer 1963), "Fact and Mystery: Flannery O'Connor" (*Commonweal,* December 6, 1963). For that matter, this writer herself followed what might be termed the

party line—a good line it was, and true—"Four Stories of
Flannery O'Connor" (*Thought,* Autumn 1962). But we all
missed something vital; something that Flannery told us so
plainly: that the ability to write is not only a gift from God but
a vocation, and "a vocation" she says, "is a limiting factor which
extends even to the kind of material that the writer is able to
apprehend imaginatively." The point she was making is that a
writer may choose what he will write about but he cannot choose
what he is able to make come alive. And herein lies the factor
that made so many critics stumble. Vocation is not an easy thing
to understand. Someday when space is not a problem this writer
would like to study Flannery in light of her God-given vocation.
I would wish that I might have done this while she was living,
for Flannery and I came to be friends, and once she turned to me
at a time she was deeply and grossly misunderstood—and
calumniated. . . .

But now Flannery is gone. What is written is written. Even
as Yahweh "raised the needy from the dust and lifted up the
the poor man from the dunghill" so did Flannery's creative
genius, through her own sense of vocation, take the hard baked
red clay of her native Georgia to make of it minor literary im-
mortals. In discussing the constant accusation that she was preoccupied with the grotesque, the freaks of human nature rather
than normal people, Flannery said earnestly, "Sister, I write
about grotesque people because I write about them best. It is
my vocation to write about Redemption, and when one sees life
from that viewpoint one sees so many distortions in today's
world that are accepted as normal and natural. To people who so
accept distortions (as natural and normal) you have to exagger-
ate your point."

Flannery O'Connor was not an easy person to draw into
protracted conversation about her work. But once I saw her
face light up with an inner radiance, almost, one would say, with
the joy of discovery. We were discussing Tarwater in particular,
and in general, why *The Violent Bear It Away* was not as success-

ful as some of her stories. "They didn't understand it," I said, "they did not get the point. They were too concerned with details . . ." This was when her face lighted up. "But, oh, I have had my complete fulfillment today," she said. "One of the young Sisters here at Marillac College told me that she 'read Tarwater loud and clear: I understand him perfectly! He was struggling with his vocation. I've been through that—I know just how he felt and you did, too.' " Pensive for a moment, Flannery smiled at me: "You couldn't ask more from any reader than that, now could you?"

5

The Place of Religious in Social Work

The part played by the parochial school system in the growth, spread, solidity and fruitfulness of the Church in the United States can scarcely be overestimated. But side by side with the apostolate of education we find the apostolate of charity, for charity has ever been the most compelling and irresistible form of apologetics. "By this shall all men know that you are My disciples: that you have love one for another." This love did not permit religious Brothers and Sisters, originally intended for educational work, to ignore the orphans, the plague-stricken, the helpless infant and the hopeless aged. In the early annals of our pioneer communities, one can only guess, from sparsely kept records, where the work of education merged with, or extended itself to, the field of charity. It is not necessary to do so. A panoramic view of the United States, even a hundred years ago, would show many sections dotted by institutions of mercy as well as by churches and schools, all speaking of "Faith that worketh by charity." The agnostics of France flung at Ozanam the taunt, "Show us your works." Never could that taunt be used against American Catholics.

From the very beginning, the Church in the United States, drawing its strength from the millions of Catholic immigrants who came to its shores, became entrenched in the field of charity—a power recognized as such, and one to be dealt with respectfully. For the building and maintenance of its charitable institutions, the Church depended not so much upon the financial generosity of its members, as upon the enduring endowment of Brothers and Sisters who consecrated their lives to the service of their suffering fellow men, because they accepted literally the words of our Lord: "Whatsoever you do to the least of Mine, that you do unto Me."

Apprentice training was the accepted method of education and training for these services, even as it was, to a large extent, for teachers up to a century ago, and for nurses until fifty years ago. Nothing was farther from the thoughts of religious stationed in orphanages, infant asylums, homes for delinquent girls, settlements for overall service, and other such institutions, than that some day they would need collegiate degrees; that they would be enrolled in university courses, not only to improve their services, but in order to retain their place in the field of charity.

The dictum "No man is an island" applies with overpowering force to an institution set up to meet the social needs of man. Such institutions, Catholic and non-Catholic, suddenly found the tidal wave of Public Welfare lapping at their foundations. The wave, which began as a trickle in the way of almshouses and poor farms after the Elizabethan manner, became a torrent of Federal-State-Local Relief, highly organized, tax-supported and politically powerful. This necessitated a vast increase of federal and state employees, the necessity being heavily augmented by the relief programs following the First World War, the Great Depression, and the inception of Social Security. This, in turn, pointed up the need of a special body of knowledge and skills necessary to the handling of human problems. One had to understand not only the people coming for aid, but also the problems that created that need. One had to understand how to solve problems not only on a transient basis, but on one that would be wise and permanent. The problems posed were sometimes individual, sometimes arising from a family situation, sometimes environmental factors. Each called for a diifferent set of tools and techniques.

SOCIAL WORK AS A PROFESSION

Thus persons, both paid and volunteer, engaged in the field of social welfare, sought a common knowledge that would serve both as precept and practice in the type and kind of services they were called upon to render. As there was no such body of knowledge available, the universities to which prospective students appealed, borrowed from established fields of discipline for curriculum construction. They drew upon psychology to tell how to deal with various personalities of different age and cultural background; they drew upon psychiatry and sociology for insight into what seemed to be aberrations in temperament and behavior; they drew upon law to understand legal complications, and upon medicine to comprehend the effects of illness upon social and familial relations. From these sources the universities sought, often in rather eclectic fashion, to compound a profession—the profession of social work.

Concurrently with this educational flood, so to speak, that had to be reckoned with by charitable institutions, there was an ebbing of financial support. War Chests (1914-1918) gave such relief from multiple solicitations that they became permanent under the title of Community Chests (within the last two years changed to United Fund) with one annual drive for all non-tax-supported social agencies. This gradually—or rather not so gradually—replaced private charity and personal donations to Catholic agencies, so that these agencies became to a large extent dependent upon allocations from the Community Chest for their very existence, and for the conditions of their functioning. In quick succession, then, came these three factors affecting vitally the work of religious in the field of charity: first, the acceptance of social work as a profession; second, the consequent standardization of both employees and the agencies in which they worked; third, state supervision of both private and public institutions, to insure compliance with the standards imposed.

It was not a bad thing, this setting up of standards for social agencies; as a matter of fact, it was a very good thing, but it came so quickly that most communities were unprepared to adjust to it with trained personnel from their own membership. And whereas major superiors, in most instances, grasped the situation and approved of the changes demanded, they could not, overnight, "sell" the idea to the Sisters staffing the institutions. Conservatism, so often the bulwark of religious communities, in this instance worked against them. The only recourse open was to employ lay social workers and have them take over what up to then had been considered the sacred functions of Brothers and Sisters dedicated to serve in orphanages, probationary or reform schools, settlements and institutions for infants and for the aged. What had been hitherto regarded as simple and routine procedures suddenly bristled with complexities. The lay social workers did the preplacement investigations, the intake service, the counseling. They made the decisions for removal of children from the institution and for foster home care. Obviously, this created a situation which no amount of tact on one side or devotion on the other could free from misunderstandings, suspicions and resentments. This was an unavoidable and transient period, which could well be passed over in silence, save that it made both superiors and Sisters look upon education for social work quite differently from the view they took of education for teaching and nursing. Certainly, as we shall see later, their first reaction was not to send the Sisters in great numbers for social work degrees. But in this Providence took a hand. If even today social work education is so uncertain of its aims and goals as to call forth such articles as "Social Work: Profession Chasing Its Tail" (*Harper's,* March 1957), it is all to the good that Brothers and Sisters did not, twenty years ago, rush headlong in pursuit of an M.A. in that somewhat confused field.

PROFESSIONAL PREPARATION IN SOCIAL WORK

Nevertheless, religious engaged in these services were forced to reappraise their duties. Dedication to the works of mercy did not, of itself, give professional competency, nor could selfless devotion substitute for scientific knowledge. There was much more to child-rearing than custodial care. Disturbed children needed more than maternal solicitude; not by bread alone did the rejected child live or take on new courage. Religious superiors were brought face-to-face with the fact that great strides had been made in child study, in geriatrics, in the psychology of the unwed mother, in adoption principles and procedures, in social organization and administration, and about these things the Sisters had but an experiential knowledge—a kind of trial-and-error method of handling problems, and one that did not always contribute to the well-being of the client. Superiors saw, that just as once they had been forced, first by their own recognition of the need, and second by the pressures placed upon them by regional and state accrediting agencies, to give opportunities for higher education to their teachers and nurses, so the time had come when adequate preparation for Sisters assigned to social work was a *must*.

It was a fact hard to accept in the way that it came. College education had been a more gradual thing for teachers; even yet there are states that do not require the baccalaureate as the minimum preparation. But for the social work degree, the baccalaureate was the prerequisite; the master in social work was the requirement for the casework services that hitherto had been administered by Sisters with, in many instances, less than a high school education. Religious superiors saw no help but to advise their Sisters to accept wholeheartedly the services lay-workers rendered, to work through and with Catholic Charities and other supporting bureaus, and to do their best in meeting accrediting standards by hiring lay help, while they turned their attention to long-range planning for social work education for their Sisters.

EDUCATIONAL PROBLEMS

That they were slow in assigning Sisters to university education in social work was due to two factors: first, the candidates had to be selected and assigned to colleges to earn the bachelor's degree; second, there are in the country only six Catholic schools of social service. The bachelor's requirements in these, as well as in secular universities, were then and are still in so fluid a state as to permit almost any kind of undergraduate background to qualify for what should be a very solid professional super-structure at the master's level. This probably has brought about the comment that today, social workers—despite their profes-sional degree (M.S.W.)—are among the least academically edu-cated people the universities graduate. From the Catholic view-point this is tragic, especially where religion, philosophy and theology have not been given due place. For no one comes closer to being called upon to do the work of a priest than does a social worker, who, by her profession, must counsel the doubtful, instruct the socially and morally ignorant, help people make profound decisions about their personal and familial life, and enter into problems so intimately connected with the moral welfare of clients that one might truthfully say that social workers cannot escape either promoting or jeopardizing the salvation of souls.

SECULARISM AND SOCIAL WORK

Now it is the contention of this writer that it is the end of Catholic social work to save souls, or social work has no reason for its existence within the framework of Catholic education. Oddly enough, this is a statement that will be denied even by Catholic social workers. To quote Father Brogan of the Catholic Charities in Chicago, "In general, social work has made religion an adjunct, whereas for Catholic social workers it should be its very life. Casework has added Catholicity as a sort of seventh veil to cover and disguise some of its completely naturalistic concepts."[1] He adds an ominous warning: "If we permit the

---

[1]Rev. Bernard Brogan, "In-Service Training for Catholic Social Work," *Proceedings, 38th National Conference of Catholic Charities* (September 1952), pp. 112-17.

salvation of souls to be obscured and neglected in our anxiety to build up a scientific and naturalistic attitude towards the needs of others, Catholic social work will quickly and entirely die." It would be an interesting quotation to bring up in a casework class at practically any one of our Catholic schools of social work— even where the instructor is a Catholic; very often they are not Catholics, for the reason that Catholic teacher-shortage is perhaps nowhere more acute than in our own schools of social work. And, but too often, where there is a Catholic instructor in such key classes as casework, psychiatry, human welfare, he or she has been educated at a non-Catholic university.

This thought alone prompts sober reflection on the proximate danger to the Catholic philosophy of one educated in a completely secular atmosphere. If social work instructors in Catholic schools have themselves been educated in secular institutions they will have been exposed to naturalism and materialism; if they have escaped these influences entirely, it will only be through heroic efforts of their own.

Further, if these social work instructors in Catholic schools, themselves educated in secular institutions, are priests or religious, they may have been previously prepared to evaluate what was presented to them, and to make a new and orthodox synthesis of their own, to pass on to their students. To assume that this would always, or even frequently, be done, is truly—an assumption. If they are lay persons, it is possible that they have made these adaptations and purifications, but it is not probable. If they are non-Catholic, the chance of their doing so is remote indeed.

As matters stand today, the social work profession is almost wholly in the hands of lay persons educated in secular universities. As for Sisters, a cursory glance at the numbers graduating from our Catholic universities (and this does not imply that all graduates are Catholic) shows Sisters to be in a negligible minority. (See Table I.)

TABLE 1: CATHOLIC SCHOOLS OF SOCIAL WORK

SCHOOL	DATE ESTABLISHED (Given by the School)	RELIGIOUS GRADUATES		LAY GRADUATES	
		Priests	*Nuns*	*Cath.*	*Non-Cath.*
Boston College	1936	7	10	524	41
Fordham University	1929	(not given)	57	700	123
Catholic University	1947	47	56	318	86
Worden School	1950	0	0	23	32
St. Louis University	1934	9	28	317	28
Loyola University	1938	28		282	122

Obviously, there are too few Sisters in the field. Hundreds of Catholic charitable institutions for children, for the aged, for the needy of all kinds, are still administered by religious. The public automatically associates Sisters with these works. By their high motivation it is fitting that they should take the lead where suffering and social ills abound. But let us not blink at the disturbing fact that the works of mercy—now organized as a profession—are more than eighty percent in the hands of lay persons. Even in the Catholic sector the Sisters do not have the influence they should have by reason of ownership and administration, nor by reason of their complete dedication to this apostolate.

For purposes of comparison, let us list the graduates of six secular schools of social work, which will point up in sharper focus the fact that what should be a profession par excellence for Sisters is, in reality, almost entirely in the hands of seculars.

The full impact of these figures comes home when we view them from a comparative angle. They show that fewer than 200 Sisters have received degrees in social work from Catholic universities in the last 30 years. Transfer those same figures for the moment to the field of general education. Ask yourself what would be the state of our high schools and colleges if within 10 years, fewer than 200 Sisters had earned the master's degree.[2]

---

[2] A 1956 Sister Formation Survey counts 10,925 teaching Sisters with M.A. degrees.

TABLE 2: NON-CATHOLIC SCHOOLS OF SOCIAL WORK

SCHOOL	DATE ESTABLISHED (Given by the School)	TOTAL GRADUATES	APPROX. NO. OF CATHOLICS
University of Chicago	1920	2,375	15% - 20%
U. of Southern Calif.	1920	*412	20%
Western Reserve	1916	1,701	Unknown
U. of California	1947	137	"
Washington U. (St. Louis)	1927	726	"
U. of Calif. (Berkeley)	1944	697	"

*Figures given are for the past ten years only.

What would be the state and standing of our institutions of education? Of our hospitals? It is so preposterous that we consider it unthinkable. But what would have happened in the field of general education has happened in the field of charity with its multiple works of mercy. Charitable deeds testify to the divinity of the Church's doctrine and dogma. Yet into them secularism has not stealthily crept—rather it has marched in boldly, frankly challenging the Church's right to have any part therein save on sufferance. Read the reiterated warnings of the hierarchy at every annual Convention of Catholic Charities, and one will soberly conclude that in the twentieth century, secularism offers the same threat to charity, that Jansenism, in the seventeenth century, offered to faith.

PRIESTS EDUCATED IN SOCIAL WORK

If only religious superiors of women's communities had shared the awareness and vision of the Episcopate in this matter, and followed in their lead! Noting the trend of the times, the Bishops not only set up diocesan bureaus of Catholic Charities, but they sent priests to Catholic and to secular universities to obtain the master's degree in social work, so that all offices would have qualified and competent directors of Catholic Charities. These offices, staffed preponderantly by lay women, a good number of them not Catholic, are calling for qualified Sisters. Some communities have responded by giving them Sisters, and the directors are loud in their praise of the Sisters' work within the office and in their field of casework and supervision. The directors continue to call for more Sisters. If only religious communities will "stop, look, and listen," if they will keep what may well be termed a rendezvous with destiny, every Catholic Charities office may yet become a bastion of charity, even as our schools are now bastions of faith.

Finances? There are probably more scholarships for Sisters available in this field than one supposes. But apart from scholarships, 500 Sisters could be educated for the master's degree at less than construction cost and equipment for one ordinary modern child-serving institution. In past years, communities deemed it necessary to invest millions in orphanages, homes for the aged, infant and maternity agencies . . . (whence comes the odious and timeworn expression "vested interests" hurled at every institution by lay supervisors who consider them the "last resort" for the indigent and dependent). Did we but now spend one tithe of that money to provide well-educated religious to work, under the direction of the Bishops, to maintain and advance the Church's place in the field of charity, what a difference it would make. More and more the state is providing material aid for the underprivileged citizen: the dependent child, the unwed mother and her infant, the handicapped, the aged, the unemployed. Unless Sisters are accepted now as competent and qualified administrators and workers within the framework of state fund programs, serving under proper episcopal authority, while the field is not yet defined or delimited, it will be taken for granted that they have no proper place in it.

THE NEED FOR RELIGIOUS IN SOCIAL WORK

But Sister social workers are needed not only in our institutions and agencies, not only in Catholic Charities offices. They are needed and have a contribution to make in every phase of

service. Let us get them into these services while their presence
there is not only acceptable, but eagerly sought. Sister social
workers should be in schools, in hospitals, in public health;
they should represent the Church and defend its interest and
philosophy on boards, committees, local, state, and national
councils. Above all, Sister social workers of education and
experience should be on the faculties of universities to help combat the naturalistic attitudes and mere humanitarian philosophies.
By their standing and competency they should make the Church's
influence felt in national organizations, and by their contributions
to social work literature, strengthen the leaven of Catholicity, and
give the supernatural its due recognition. To bring this about,
money is a negligible factor; vision, courage, and daring are of
the essence.

As a matter of fact and record, the social field itself needs
Sisters, with all they could bring to it, almost as much as the
Church itself needs more religious. With charity founded on
faith, Sisters would bring to social work a clarity of purpose which
its acknowledged leaders say is sorely lacking. Read secular literature and search in vain for so much as a definition of social
work. Listen to recognized authorities in the field: "Both social
work and social workers should be looked upon as evolving
concepts that are as yet too fluid for precise definition."[3] Isn't
it a bit odd to belong to a profession one cannot define? Yet
this same inability to define clearly what one is and what one
does is stressed by another leader in the field: "Social work, like
the sciences, may find that the last thing it will know, is what it
is all about."[4] Much of the literature reveals a stating and a
restating of motives, purposes, goals, a seeking after definitions,
that—for the Catholic—grow pale before the Church's literal
acceptance of Christ's words: "Whatsoever you do unto the

---

[3]Hollis and Taylor, *Social Work Education in the United States* (New
York: Columbia Press, 1951), p. 54.

[4]M. A. Gannon, "Guiding Motives in Social Work," *New Directions in
Social Work*. Ed. Cora Kasius (New York: Harper Brothers, 1954), p. 13.

least of Mine, you do unto Me." Here we have the motive, the purpose, the goal. In these words we have the all-embracing definitition of social work. The client is Christ. The motive is Christ. The goal is Christ. And here we have the practical exemplification that just as there is a philosophical and theological basis for Catholic doctrine and education, so there is a philosophical and theological basis for Catholic social work.

More than at any time before, Sisters are needed to restore Christ to the field. A secularist reading that line (even a Catholic secularist) would frown and say, "But social work is not an apostolate like missionary work; it takes much more than religion to solve the problems that are brought to us every day; there can no more be a 'Catholic way' of looking at social work than a 'Catholic way' of looking at dentistry." And, not so much as an afterthought, either, but as a quite emphatic forethought, would come the inevitable: "And social work with its problems of morality, its need to plumb the depths of human miseries often stemming from sin and malice, are neither the *métier* nor the *milieu* for religious—these constitute the layman's world, and clients feel more at home discussing their problems with lay-people than with Sisters."

It is an assumption, of course, sometimes tacitly, more often openly, expressed even by Catholics. But is the assumption justified? Has it been thought through? Certainly, it needs to be carefully and objectively examined.[5] The difference between a lay social worker and a Sister is not in the accidents of dress, residence or rule of life. It lies within the essentials that constitute her "state"—the holy vows of religion: poverty, chastity, and obedience. These vows are aimed at minimizing and keeping wholly in check the threefold concupiscence of the eyes, the flesh, and the pride of life. Now it is patent that social ills and evils are rooted, directly or indirectly, individually or environmentally, personally or collectively, in these three concupiscences.

---

[5]It might be interesting to compare the information given to Sisters in confidential records with what lay workers receive from the same client.

It would be logical, then, to assume that a person particularly armed against them would be peculiarly well fitted to be their adversary. Dedication and consecration to Christ insure an all-out effort as well as a special strength to reproduce His life on earth. What was His public life but one long service to the under-privileged? He so identified Himself socially with sinners that it was made a reproach to Him: "If He knew what manner of woman this is that touches Him." . . . "They bring to Him one taken in adultery." . . . And we know that for this woman He had words of encouragement and advice. Mary Magdalene became by Christ's own appointment the close companion of Mary Immaculate. Obviously, consecration to Christ does not imply isolation from the problem of sin and its consequences.

INFLUENCE OF RELIGIOUS SOCIAL WORKERS

Prescinding for a moment from the spiritual, the superior excellence of the religious social worker is evident from a psychological point of view. What does a client, adolescent, adult, or aged (always insecure in himself), seek in a counselor? Security. A manifest, serene security is the *sine qua non* on which confidential rapport is based. Who has security to a greater degree than a religious? Freed from the economic, social, and emotional stresses that are an inevitable part of lay life, a Sister has the unshaken security deriving from the vow of obedience. Her habit proclaims to the world that she has found a meaning to life, and a way of living it, that are, to her, satisfactory to the highest possible degree. There is a conscious or unconscious inference on the part of the client that one who has been eminently successful in solving life's problems for herself may be skilled in solving life's problems for others. Again, rapport between Sister and client is almost always automatically established. The client need not strain to catch or remember the name, since the word "Sister" suffices for both social (in the sense of professional) and friendly purposes. A Sister's habit betokens help and service as instantly as does the uniform of police or fireman. A needy person knows that a Sister pursues her profession of social work as a way of life and not as a means of livelihood. This, in itself, establishes a different type of rapport not possible to the lay worker.

I have no intention of minimizing the high caliber work done by lay people in the social field. Indeed—and perhaps this should have been said sooner—I am among the most ardent advocates for the view that more Catholic men and women should go into the social work profession; that, where the interests of the Church require, and circumstances permit, they team up with religious to do the Church's work. Such teamwork is done extensively in the hospital field; it has now become a "must" in the educational field, and it should and can be seen at its best in the social field, That this may be accomplished, professional social workers must find—as teachers and nurses have found—a large number of Sisters belonging to their associations, appearing on their programs, understanding and advancing the interest of their common profession. An entire article could easily be written on the specific areas of service open to Catholic lay workers. How greatly are they needed in tax-supported agencies, federal, state and local (obviously closed to religious), that the leaven of their Catholic principles may lighten the load of public relief. In civic and social projects, on philanthropic boards and committees, they can make their influence felt. A certain Archbishop told me recently that his "right arm" was a social worker who held an important position with the State Welfare Department. He said that she was an employee of the local Catholic Charities when the offer of a position with the State was made to her, and that she had asked his advice about accepting. "Take it," he urged, "take it by all means. You will do the Church a greater service there than here." Then, to me, he added, "I would not have said that, had she not been one of our finest Catholics."

But this essay is directed to Sisters, and is engaged in refuting the assumption that, by their life of consecration and devotion, Sisters are not equipped to do social work. Specifically, there is that oft-repeated statement, not borne out by facts, that clients feel more at home in relating their troubles to lay people than to Sisters. Always, of course, there will be individual exceptions. But it is certainly a gratuitous assertion to say that Sisters—because of their religious profession—cannot, as ably as lay workers meet and help solve the problems posed by clients who seek alleviation from trials that oppress them.

SOCIAL PROBLEMS

The problems do run the whole gamut of moral misery. Will poverty and its accompanying privations for hordes of hungry children be alleviated by planned parenthood? What does one say to a woman who, in desperation, answers a landlord's threat of eviction with the promise that her fourteen-year-old daughter may meet him "at the corner tonight"—if only he will wait another month for the rent? How does one best handle the guilt-ridden unwed mother, seventeen years old—or the one who will be forty-one her next birthday? How does one help this unwed mother to decide the poignant question of retaining the child to bring up as her own, or to relinquish it for adoption to a desirable couple? May a wife divorce her husband who she finds is taking dope and giving it to their son? These are everyday problems brought to social service clinics.

And within children's institutions, how can we help Anne, nearing her fifteenth birthday, to face reality and square up to accepting the fact that her mother is promiscuous, and therefore that it is unwise and even dangerous for her to spend a weekend at home? How can we get little Jackie to stop threatening to kill the man he knows to have supplanted his father in a home that was once happy? How does one help rebuild the life of a little girl who has been the victim of her own parents' unscrupulous dishonesty? How does one handle the adolescent who pledges revenge on a society that discriminated against him because of his color, creed or heritage?

THE VOWS OF RELIGIOUS AID SOCIAL WORK

These are not problems to occupy the minds of consecrated souls, say those who have a strange way of interpreting the parable of the lost sheep. Lay people—they aver—can do better counseling here because they are closer to the heart of the matter. We have said that the essential difference between the lay worker and religious is the total oblation by vow on the part of religious. Do the holy vows, then, unfit religious for the service of the poor? The very practice of poverty, required of a Sister by her first vow, gives her an at-homeness with her client that completely obviates envy. Actually, poverty allows her to identify with the poorest of the poor. The client will not eye her dress with cynical suspicion; she has no possessions to arouse envy, no worldly social position to create a void between her and the one who seeks her help. Actually, a Sister's experiential knowledge of non-possession gives her a real empathy with her client. The spendthrift housewife, squandering a meager income on luxuries, will readily accept budget control from one who speaks objectively and with a detachment born of experience, of the judicious spending of money. The boy caught with a stolen car, the girl with shoplifted finery, will unabashedly "talk it over" with Sister, since she, too, belongs to the have-nots. The client's confused sense of values derives clarification from the simplification and unification seen in a Sister's "deprived" life.

Now the strongest protests against a Sister's suitability for social work are based on her vow of chastity—what it prescribes and what it prohibits. But do the obligations of her vow of chastity unfit her for dealing with moral evils and their consequences? No more, it would seem, than does perfect physical health unfit a nurse for dealing with the plague-stricken. For the chastity demanded of a religious in the active life is less faithfully symbolized by a "polished mirror which the least breath will tarnish" than by the sun's rays which penetrate the foulest places, dispelling the noisomeness there without contracting the slightest taint.

Her vow of obedience gives weight and wisdom to her words when she reminds a derelict client of the marriage vows, of the promises made in the Sacrament of Matrimony. Her own living under a rule of obedience makes intelligent to youth what she says concerning their need to live in harmony with authority. The prisoner, the woman "on parole," the child who has run away from home, all sense that Sister, too, has to play the game the way the rules are written.

SISTER FORMATION ESSENTIAL

So a religious then whose every act becomes, by reason of her vows, an act of religion, has high potentialities as a social worker. But her qualifications and gifts remain only potentialities unless, through preparation, formation, and education of a very special kind, they are synthesized and made ready for the work at hand, just as the potentialities that lie inherent in a piece of mahogany must be brought out by skilled craftsmanship before a valuable piece of furniture can be produced. In a word, religious entering the field of social work have need of a sound and solid education, the liberating, widening, enlarging, steel undergirding of a special curriculum, with good sequences in philosophy, theology, psychology, and social science. At the baccalaureate level it should be in every and in the best sense of the word, a truly *liberal* education. Only such a foundation can make fruitful the professional subject matter and field work that are the core of the master's program. This undergraduate work should be, in itself, *Sister Formation* as well as *Social Worker Formation,* so integrating and welding knowledge with practice, *being* with *doing,* that the Sister-student comes from the experience not so much informed as *formed;* not so much a person who knows what ought to be done, as one *who does what needs doing* with capable prudence, knowledge and fortitude. For one of the ends to be kept in mind in educating Sisters for social work is that they may be prepared also to teach social workers—and a teacher instructs more by what she *is* than through the subject matter she teaches.

To this writer, a member of a multiple-works community, no better foundation could be laid for the superstructure of higher-level professional education in the field of social work than an adaptation of the undergraduate curriculum prepared at the Everett Workshop of 1956. One could recommend this same preparation for the lay social work student, with its excellent inclusion of philosophy and theology as the instrumental basis and integrating principle for the studies in the behavioral and professional sciences that are to follow. Lay workers may object to any suggestion that recommends moral theology as a part of the curriculum. They are quick to assert that their profession, with its distinctive body of knowledges and skill, must not be "confused" with religion.

There need be no confusion. There is nothing that religion will prescribe that is not sound psychology and social wisdom. Our Catholic religion prescribes, for example, that there be no attempt at artificial birth control. Psychology teaches us to beware of creating guilt feelings in the client—that nothing is so deleterious to his emotional and psychological happiness as feelings of unworthiness and self-contempt. Yet these very feelings are engendered in any sane person who willfully misuses or abuses a God-given faculty that has its own intrinsic purpose and ideal use. Even if no principles of religion were involved in artificial birth control, it would still be unsound casework to recommend its practice to clients, and, of course, no truly Catholic social worker would, however difficult it may be for poverty-stricken groups to have large families. The pagan code gives as much space to the virtue of temperance as does our own religious code—for a different motive, of course.

RELIGION AND PSYCHOLOGY

Religion teaches us conformity to God's will; but sound psychology endeavors to help us get along with our environment and to avoid frustrations. Nothing so enlightens the mind and brings to it peace and acceptance of the inevitable as does the doctrine of divine Providence. But why must this idea be placed on a merely natural level? We seldom deal with atheists. The idea of our heavenly Father's solicitude is not repugnant even to non-Catholic clients. The Beatitudes are not out of their sphere of understanding. This is not to make religion an opiate, but rather a healing, inspiring philosophy of life—a bulwark against life's warfare and the sudden changes of fortune.

We have said that no Catholic lay worker would recommend, in her casework, the violation of any social principles laid down by God or the Church's law. But a second glance at the statistics of this article will show that Catholic lay workers are outnumbered in the field by more than three times as many non-Catholic lay workers. (And remember there are fifty times as many lay workers as there are religious!) This gives pause to our thinking when we ask, whither Catholic social work, whither the works of mercy?

The answer must inevitably lead us back to the thesis of this essay—there is dire need of more Sisters in the field of social work. Will religious communities answer the plea of Bishops and priests who everywhere recognize this need? Practically, let us pose the question: Are we to consider the education of youth and the care of the sick, as represented by the vast network of schools and hospitals, as something to be held at all costs, financial and otherwise, something sacred to be defended against encroachment, and allow the other works of mercy, the Church's boast and glory down the ages, to perish by default?

At the risk of playing the role of a voice crying in the wilderness, I make two statements: first, the works of mercy need not be lost to us if religious communities will even now awaken to the need of preparing and forming more Sisters for these works, even as they prepare and form their Sisters for teaching and for nursing; second, the works of mercy will inevitably diminish and depart from our care if Sister-recruits are not educated in large numbers and sent to aid our Bishops, priests, and lay workers, struggling against secularizing influences, to retain these works under truly Catholic auspices. Could Bishops, priests, and lay teachers alone have built up our splendid Catholic school system? Could Bishops, priests, and lay nurses alone have maintained the high status of our Catholic hospitals? Can Bishops, priests and lay social workers alone preserve our Catholic social agencies?

6

Who Is Sick Among Us?

I

It is a phenomenon that 183,000 Sisters, a very small segment of the approximately 47 million Catholics in the United States, should attract so much attention from press and pulpit, radio and television. This attention is not confined to Catholics. If we may judge by journals of opinion whose combined circulation reaches tens of millions, non-Catholics too, are avidly interested. The tone of most of the publicity is analytical and critical, adverse and advisory. To what purpose this large-scale scrutiny? Why did it originate, to what end is it tending and what seem to be its effects?

Those most immediately affected, Sisters themselves, may well pause and ask the question: What is wrong with religious life? Is it, as many critics both cleric and lay have suggested, finished? Is it a relic, like the Index, of something that once served a useful purpose but is no longer needed? Or should the question be, not "What is wrong with religious life," but rather "What ails religious life?" There is a definite difference between being wrong and being sick. Many aspects of modern living are sick. It might well be admitted that religious life today is sick. But what is the cause?

A medical diagnosis has to deal with the negative as well as with the positive. A physical checkup often reveals the presence of "foreign bodies" that must be removed before a more positive step toward a buildup of health can be taken. Often it is as important to know what not to do as it is to arrive at a formula of what must be done.

Assuming that religious life is truly ailing—few will dispute that—the first step toward a diagnosis and remedial agents is to study the symptoms: these are a marked restlessness among Sisters, many defections, much confusion brought on by uncertainty and ambivalence toward changes in the Church, disdain for the past, instability, resentment of authority, lack of trust in anyone but their peers, a continuous challenge of the validity of the "call" of vocation.

For some Sisters recommended changes in religious life are coming too slowly; for others, change is coming too fast. For the more perceptive of all groups, the changes being made seem all too often to deal with minor matters, *petit détails,* rather than with major issues.

The situation of the Church today and, by association, religious Communities, has been likened to that of the post-Reformation era. There were radical illnesses in that day that threatened the Church from within, long before the desperate pseudo-remedy of the Reformation was attempted.

A hard, objective look at what elements might be sapping contemporary religious life from within, endangering its health and vitality, would enlighten the thoughtful to unsuspected or only partially revealed ailments that pose a dangerous threat at this very hour. Even a necessarily brief research into three areas would be an effective start.

THE AFFLUENT COMMUNITY

Recently, a widely circulated secular newspaper carried an advertisement for the sale of bonds. It stated matter-of-factly: "Fifteen million dollars in bonds, paying 4½ per cent interest, is guaranteed by. . . ." Here followed the name of the religious Community—a name which, in itself, connoted dedication to absolute poverty. Quite likely few readers saw the inherent incongruity in the advertisement.

But it might well give pause to those deeply concerned with the welfare of religious Communities. Within the framework of corporate wealth, how effectively and for how long can a meaningful personal poverty be practiced? In religious Congregations,

as in other corporations, the financial nerve is highly sensitive
and reacts to the least touch. Justifications for corporate wealth
rush to its defense. Arguments are drawn from logic, economics
and sociology. The laws of prudence, understanding and justice
are cited. But they ring rather hollow when tested against the
words: "Go, sell what you have, give it to the poor, then come
follow Me." Nor do they solve the contradiction passively
accepted by many religious Communities: "Sisters X and Y and
Z must love and practice poverty; but the Community, composed
of Sisters X and Y and Z, must strive for and possess corporate
wealth."

St. Paul is very blunt on this point: "The desire of money is
the root of all evil." All evil. Since the Apostle makes his statement all-embracing, would we not be foolish and even hypocriti-
cal to exclude, from our research into the cause of the "ailments"
that affect Communities, this evil that is so plainly and sternly
pointed out?

COURAGEOUS DISCIPLESHIP

The first step in special, courageous discipleship enunciated
by Christ was: "Go, sell what you have, give it to the poor, then
come follow Me." Doing this corporately as well as personally
is possible in our day as never before. There is much less need
today for religious Communities to depend solely upon their own
hard work, thrift and sacrifices, together with gifts from bene-
factors, in order to alleviate the lot of the orphan and the aged,
the homeless and the unemployed, the sick and the afflicted.
Our near-Welfare State has set up a gigantic system for their
relief and annually dispenses billions of dollars in welfare funds.
Have Communities taken full cognizance of this and adjusted
their service in keeping with it? Should they not be more free
from fiancial anxieties and economic reckonings than they were
when private charity stood practically alone in the field?

Would it not be a gigantic step in renewal, and a decisive one,
if Communities changed the focus of their services, recognizing

that impersonal aid, administered by the State, is no substitute for
the charity of Christ? There is a profound implication in the
fact that the greatest riot to date, that in Watts, California,
occurred in a State where welfare benefits are the highest and
the easiest to come by. Yet when all of the facts were carefully
sifted, when the elements of unemployment, poverty, broken
families, inadequate health and educational facilities were
assessed, the Commission appointed to investigate the cause of
the riot pinned it to one thing. Welfare. Welfare aid, they stated,
robbed a person of his dignity, weakened his sense of responsibility, and sapped his moral fiber.

Here, and in other areas of Society, we find a field ripe for
the harvest. But in the face of it we have the anomaly of Sisters,
with a Vow of Poverty, teaching in schools from which children
who cannot pay tuition are barred, nursing in hospitals where
ability to pay, personally or through insurance, is a condition for
admission, working in welfare agencies where the budget set
by state and civic authorities limits their services.

A Sister's personal sanctification is not the only aim of her
Vow of Poverty. Her own sanctification is contingent on how far
her neighbors are benefited, corporally, and spiritually, by her
vows. Here is truly a field for courageous, heroic renewal. When
ways and means are found to give a Sister's vow of poverty
meaning beyond the realm of permissions and possessions; when
she can feel that because of it she has a oneness with the afflicted,
the destitute and the deprived, which enables her to lighten their
burdens while strengthening their self-respect, she will experience
the fullness of her dedication. Then, indeed, will her "anxious
wavering" cease. But this can be accomplished only when the
dichotomy between personal and corporate poverty has been
abolished.

DANGER OF IGNORING INTANGIBLES

Religious women are still largely institutionally based. Income
and expense can be readily totaled, and the success of an institution is very largely reckoned by its financial holdings. Intangible

values, which are the very basis of the religious life, cannot be data processed. The real danger of their loss of appeal must not be ignored. If the Community as a corporate body does not place them first, how long will the individual Sister do so?

Allied to this matter is the charge, largely a just one, that Sisters in general do not know the value or even the price of material things and are oblivious to the cost of living which presses even on the moderately well-to-do. In a laudable effort to correct this, Communities have sought a concrete way in which to make Sisters aware of daily living expenses in order that they may have factual knowledge of the plight of the poor. But the approach should deal with the general rather than with the particular: monthly food bills, utilities, salaries, maintenance, and also unusual expenditures. It is conceivable that if the electric light bill, for one example, were posted each month on the Community room bulletin board the members of this particular convent household just might possibly emulate President Johnson in turning off lights in empty rooms. There are other good examples that could be offered, all in the realm of the practice of corporate poverty.

No good purpose would seem to be served, however, by showing a Sister bills for personal expenses: clothing, medicines, hospital care, education, travel, and other such items. No norm can be established in these matters since they vary from Sister to Sister and she has little control over them. Further, and more important, instead of maturing her insight into the practice of personal poverty it could very well lead to her evaluating—perhaps unwittingly—her own services by the "income and expense" yardstick. This would precipitate the Sister into a way of thinking that would threaten her whole religious life.

Bearing very directly on the matter of corporate poverty are the words found in the *Decree on the Adaptation and Renewal of Religious Life:* "Due regard being had for local conditions, religious Communities should readily offer a quasi-collective witness to poverty, and gladly use their own goods for other needs of the Church and the support of the poor whom all religious

should love after the example of Christ." Obedience to the
Church in this matter does not lie with the individual religious;
it rests in the corporate body. There is no implication here that
Communities should either close or radically change their institutions but it does suggest the wisdom of a stern and forthright
reappraisal in terms of corporate poverty. The Church has
thrown down the gauntlet in unmistakable words. Which Communities will take it up?

II

CHARACTER OF CANDIDATES AND THEIR COUNSELORS

Communities have, generally speaking, markedly increased
their sifting and selection of candidates. This firm stand, coming
at a time when applications to Sisterhoods are at an extremely
low ebb, while opening avenues of service are at full tide, is
admirable—and farsighted. It is proof that Sisters have learned
well the lesson taught by the Lord to Gideon when He showed
him that victory depended not on numbers but on faith in God.
It is proof also that Communities have a sound understanding
of current conditions, those that are obvious and others that are
subtle, which could lead a girl to think, mistakenly, that she
has a religious vocation.

Superiors, and those responsible for vocation-counseling,
recognize that the religious life with its economic and social
security can be very attractive to neurotic young women in search
of freedom from the confusion and tension of today's world. It
can also hold out to adolescents just finishing high school a
refuge from feelings of social inadequacy and a solution for
the vague sense of failure and fear of responsibility that so
often haunt young people, even those capable of impressive academic achievement. It may well be that certain resentful and
rebellious youth, who are highly but unsuccessfully competitive,
might see in the religious life bright opportunity to "get away
from it all" by choosing a vocation that will give the impression
of having gone on to "higher things."

Communities have rightly adopted the principle and policy of exercising great care and prudence in the admission of candidates. They thus hope to insure the acceptance of only normal, well-adjusted, intelligent young adults capable of being led to a full understanding of the religious life and the meaningful application of its Vows. Superiors rightly believe that only stable candidates who give promise of developing into full maturity as effective religious, who can place the love of God and love of their fellow man in perspective and in correct complementary relationships, can continue the healthy vigor of religious life.

WHO HAS FAILED?

This high degree of wisdom and prudence in the selection of candidates should result in a higher degree of perseverance. With most Communities, this has not been the case. All too frequently these carefully screened candidates, during the various stages of their religious life, are neither happy postulants, fervent novices, secure Junior Sisters nor mature religious devoted to their Community's apostolate. The question arises: Have they failed the Community or has the Community failed them?

Of course there can be no clear-cut answer to a question so heavily weighted with the human equation. But in the spirit of "What more can I do for my vineyard?" Communities might profitably examine whether the same careful thought given to the admission of postulants is carried through in the appointment of the various Mistresses who will counsel and guide them in their formative years. Prolonging these years by the establishment of Juniorates, as the Church directs, will not in itself serve the purpose intended. The all-important factor is the appointment of Mistresses who have had the special preparation and education that their duty demands. And it is precisely in this deficiency that a second symptom of illness is found.

The concept that the "good religious" will suffice for this duty and that her goodness alone will inspire others to follow her example is not tenable today. A good religious she should certainly be, but in addition she should have qualities not necessarily or even usually implied in the term. Specialization is today's key word to success. What specialization bears more directly on the welfare of Communities than the formation of their younger members? True, attention has been called to this need by those associations directly interested in the welfare of Sisters, and recommendations have been made. But it appears that this crucial matter is not generally given the priority it rates.

A thorough grounding in theology is essential—but not in itself sufficient. Mistresses at all levels should have good basic courses in psychology and proficiency in sound techniques in counseling and guidance. This will help them to take into account the blunt truth that the religious life can achieve behavioral, but not biological changes in terms of religious growth and development. The academic education of the Mistress should be liberal so that she will be thoroughly at home with collegiate pressures and problems which those in her charge will encounter. Her familiarity with current events and her interest in them will have a large bearing on the ease and confidence with which she is approached by those who need her guidance in areas seemingly having no connection with world affairs.

COMPETENT GUIDANCE NEEDED

In view of the unsettled conditions in the world, and in religious Communities today, perhaps the outstanding natural and supernatural quality that should characterize Mistresses is security. Security derives from her relations with God, and from the knowledge that she is qualified and capable of meeting the challenges of her duty. Troubles from within can effect a dangerous disturbance in Communities when members of all levels—postulants, novices and the temporarily professed—do not have the goals of their Community, and what commitment to these goals requires of them, expounded to them and presented in terms that are logically unequivocal as they are spiritually attractive.

In these days when information by catchy slogans is threatening to replace formation by serious study and self-discipline, youth is apt to embrace ideas rather than ideals. The young religious of today needs to be shown patiently, understandingly but surely, that ideas evolve into ideals only when they have stood the test of time, the crucible of suffering and the assaults of sophism. Convictions on this point can come only from the personal experiences of Mistresses who honestly accept the fact that what they are shouts much louder than what they say.

Young religious read widely—which is well—but they have not usually the discretion needed to weigh one idea against another, and to keep all within the proper hierarchy of truth and authentic values. Their avid search for self-identity, and their desire to arrive at it quickly makes it morally incumbent upon Communities to give them fully competent guides during these formative years. The little learning, which is dangerous, must be counteracted by the broad knowledge that is corrective.

Only Mistresses familiar with Holy Scripture and thoroughly acquainted with the writings of contemporary theologians can cope successfully with the free use of biblical quotations and the name-dropping of new theologians heard so frequently where junior religious foregather. To cite but a single instance: Emphasis on the Mass as a Eucharistic banquet, coupled with emphasis on the indwelling of Christ in the neighbor, has led not a few young Sisters to downgrade visits to the Blessed Sacrament, or even the making of meditation in the chapel as things that belong to a less enlightened (?) age. "If God is in my neighbor," they say, "why seek Him in the chapel or elsewhere?" The answer is that, unless we continuously seek Christ in the Eucharist, and listen to the lessons His Presence among us teaches, we will soon be quite selective about the human temples in which He is to be found. Only by a profound and loving devotion to Christ, universally present on our altars, will we be spiritually strengthened to find Him universally present in our neighbor.

SOUND PRINCIPLES ESSENTIAL

This is indeed an era of "itching ears" and of fables passing for truth. Paul's second epistle to Timothy could well be taken as a mandatory guide to all engaged in the formation and direction of young religious today. In and out of season must they preach the word. They must know how to "reprove, entreat, rebuke, in all patience and doctrine" (2 Tim. 4:2). It is imperative that Mistresses not only teach sound doctrine but that they teach it soundly and with authority. Let not fear of defections deter. Paul had his. It is significant that in the epistle just quoted Paul adds: "Demas hath left me, loving the world."

A modern Paul, the reigning Pontiff, emphasizes the need to teach sound principles:

> We must not let this obscure the important concept of the religious life, which has always been a vital notion in the Church. . . . We think it necessary to call attention once again to the inestimable value of the religious life and its vital task. This state in life, distinctively characterized by the profession of the evangelical vows, is a perfect way of life according to the teaching and example of Jesus Christ.[1]

In another context this same modern Paul points up the need for contemporary man to learn how to think in terms of God.[2] When Mistresses become proficient in teaching their charges to think in terms of God, this present generation of young Sisters will come to accept their vocation on the same terms. Then will their perseverance be assured; then will the healthy branch bear fruit.

III

THE UNCERTAIN TRUMPET

A third symptom of illness in the religious life seems to lie in a lack of courageous leadership. In the New Testament Paul warns, "If the trumpet give forth an uncertain sound, who will

---

[1] Pope Paul VI, "The Religious Life Today," Address to the General Chapters of Several Religious Orders, May 23, 1964, *The Pope Speaks,* IX, No. 4 (Spring-Summer, 1964), 398.

[2] Pastoral Letter when Archbishop of Milan, 1957.

prepare for battle?" (1 Cor. 14:8). Long before Paul the same complaint was made by Solomon: "For the deliberations of mortals are timid, and unsure are our plans" (Wis. 9:14). Timidity and fear, unsureness and uncertainty are hardly the qualities that make for confident leadership. Deliberation there must be; counsel and prudence are an indispensable preparation for action; but there is evidence today that many Sisters feel that a too prolonged deliberation is used as an excuse for delayed action. Action should be reasonably prompt and, once decided upon, the call of the trumpet must sound loud and firm. Worthy of consideration is the possibility that the "uncertain sound" emanating from indecision within the Councils of Communities today is symptomatic of a grave ailment in religious life.

The ailment appears to stem from an inability to face up fully, fairly and finally to the responsibility religious Superiors must assume in effecting the changes recommended by the Church, and then to get on with the business of making the charity of Christ known to the world—the purpose for which every Community was founded. But everywhere hesitancy abounds. There is the fear of functioning in altered conditions, and the explanation "We do not know what further changes will come" is used as a delaying tactic for putting into effect changes already implicitly decreed. A likely source of want of courage is the hesitancy to add further to the already increasing ferment in religious Communities. Here a point is missed. Ferment, within limits, is profitable and productive. It gives us bread. It gives us wine. But ferment, carried beyond its point of usefulness, spoils and destroys. Sour dough does not nourish. Vinegar does not stimulate; which points out that inaction is at times the most destructive of all courses.

DISCIPLINE INDISPENSABLE

It is time, then, to master the situations brought on by Pope John's open window. It is time to move from the less important matters, change of habit and horarium, rules and customs, to the very essential matter of the spirit of serenity and security which should typify religious life, however active its apostolate and however inevitable its tensions. Although God is not found in the whirlwind He may, at times, use one for His purpose. The present whirlwind of discontent among Sisters: the confusion of liberty with license, the continuous self-seeking demands incompatible with authentic dedication, the free dabbling in the "new theology" begetting illusions of expertise—all these factors are well calculated to make Superiors not only hesitant but downright fearful of exercising responsible authority. Perhaps the day has arrived for a bit of "counter-Reformation" which will take all the more courage, since heady ideas of "freedom" will not readily accept the logical limits of discipline. But intelligent discipline there must be if religious life is to flourish. Those who cannot accept it have no place therein.

Communities, for the most part, have long since wisely consulted all of their members as to proposed changes and listened to their spoken or written recommendations. Actually this has been going on actively for a number of years (adaptation and renewal were first urged by Pius XII in 1950), so that it would be the rare Sister today who could say that she has had no opportunity to voice her opinion. This time was necessary and commendable. But it was meant to be a transitional stage serving an acute need to update, revise or abolish archaic practices once relevant to the religious life but now either outmoded or overloaded with the accretions of years. The directives of Pius XII were simple and precise, by no means intending to invite the doubts, unrest and indecision so prevalent in Communities today. Neither is there anything in the decree on adaptation in religious life that justifies continued delay which can only engender anxiety and increase defections.

In this connection Superiors might well give thought to the effect the present stage of indecision has had and is having on postulants, novices and young Sisters. Having heard even before their admission that Communities were in considerable turmoil because of changes the Church had asked them to make; listening to Sisters debate the practicality and piety of long vocal prayers, the Community's practices and customs; the formal and informal discussions of new interpretations of the Vows—all this could easily lead these neophytes to question the wisdom of their choice. This might well be a large factor in their failure to persevere. If this state of uncertainty is to continue, it might be well for those Communities still in a state of unrest to declare a moratorium on the admission of postulants until such time as a reasonable course of action has been decided upon and a reasonable measure of certainty has solidified Community life.

How different is the effect on those Sisters, well established in the religious life, who are the bulwark of their Communities! These Sisters not only welcome change, but are spiritually gratified and intellectually grateful for the passing of formalism, traditionalism, legalism and "pietistics" which, for too long have obscured the true image of women dedicated to God, hindering a healthy growth in the spiritual life. Yet, the time of renewal and adaptation, even for such Sisters, induced pain. So much in the form of long-accustomed prayer and action, habits and attitudes grown dear through the sheer weight of unquestioning acceptance down the years had to be relinquished. It was not easy.

In adjusting to what was asked of them, to make the sacrifices entailed, seasoned Sisters called upon well-established values, particularly the value of the virtue of obedience. In doing this they grew stronger in their vocation, and their predominance in the ranks of religious is now a source of strength and reassurance.

NEW VOCABULARY—NEW CONCEPTS

But obedience (or misconceptions of obedience) is under fire today. Witness the flood of articles and books dealing with "The Crisis in Authority," "Personal Freedom and Religious Obedience," "Docility Versus Maturity," "Religious Liberty" and similar titles connoting conflict within the ranks of religious. The trend indicated by such writings should give pause to those in authority. The truth that God makes known His Will to Sisters through the medium of their Superiors stands. Now that this truth is being subjected to so many interpretations (one hears the sprightly words "holy disobedience"), it would seem to be well for Superiors to consider obedience within the context of today's spirituality. Never, perhaps, did semantics play so high a role in discussion.

Following the example of biblical scholars who, by a new wording of the sacred text, have effectively forwarded the reading of the Scriptures, Communities might well examine a terminology that is, in today's world, archaic. The term "Mother Superior" has been used for centuries. (Perhaps examination will show it to be not only archaic, but contradictory.) Mother Superior supposedly embodies the concept of what any Superior—local, provincial or general—should be. Spiritual books and conferences written for Sisters stress that Superiors should "be good mothers to the Sisters in your care." One of the highest commendations accorded a Superior is "She is so motherly!"

But the word "mother" implies children—and there's the rub. If the Superior is to be motherly, the Sisters must, perforce, be children. Thus, on one side an atmosphere of maternalism is created and, on the other side, immaturity. This is quite contrary to maternalism as exemplified in a normal, happy family, the type of family most likely to produce vocations. In such homes, young Sisters have seen "motherliness" at its best; a maternalism compassionate and understanding, and, in their young days, watchfully protective. But younger members of the family saw a subtle but steady change in the relationship between mother and older brothers and sisters. As childhood gave way to adolescence, and adolescence to young adulthood, family relationships kept pace with the biological and psychological changes. Continuing maturation was expected of them. Not only did they make personal decisions, but they participated in those affecting the family. Protectiveness gave way to confidence and trust, encouraging self-reliance and independence. Mother was still there, but as a wise, dependable resource person, and not as an omniscient power.

TERMINOLOGY AFFECTS RELATIONSHIPS

That Communities do not provide for this change in relationships (perish the compound word "superior-subject") a cursory glance at Constitutions and Rules, at spiritual books (antedating Vatican II) and other writings for Sisters will show. True, many Sisters, whether in positions of authority or not, developed into calm, courageous, self-dependent, farsighted persons; leaders within their Communities and among the laity in their respective fields of service. This they did, despite the fact that they were brought up on a spiritual diet of "Be as docile, as unquestioning when you have many years of vocation as you were the day you left the novitiate." How determined and discerning were those thousands of Sisters who grew sturdy, vigorous and secure in the face of such utterly illogical instruction. How contradictory to ask older Sisters to "look upon novices (the new) as models"!

Surely, somewhere between the extremes of a chilling superior-subject relationship, and the even more irritating one of mother-daughter, there can be found a form of interpersonal relationship that will satisfy a Sister as a woman, a Christian and a religious, whatever be her position in the Community. Is there not a form of affection that is universally satisfying yet highly individualistic? Did not Christ show us where to find this when, a few hours before His death, He bestowed upon His apostles, as an accolade, the title of "friend." "No longer do I call you servants . . . but I have called you friends" (John 15:15). In the field of friendship will be found the happy medium between maternalism and authoritarianism. Friendship sustains ideals while it equalizes persons. But this is a field all too little explored by Superiors of religious Communities. In fact, it is one in which they tread as gingerly as if it were dangerously mined.

Friendship is a talent that needs developing, a skill that must be worked at; but above all, it is a truth to be believed in, and it calls for genuine courage. It cannot be a one-way street, for the only way to have a friend is to be one. It creates particular bonds in a religious house which serve to make stronger the general bond. When a Superior is able to establish special ties of friendship with each and every Sister in the house, a spirit of friendship will permeate the entire group with admirable results. Then will the world say, "Behold those Sisters—how they love one another!"

That which authority of itself cannot command—respect, confidence and love—friendship of itself freely gives. It creates ties between persons most dissimilar in age, talents, experience and temperament; it is the open sesame to trust, loyalty, understanding and love. In true friendship is found authority without obligation, possession without proprietorship, satisfaction without selfishness. Between adults of the same sex, genuine friendship is the highest, closest tie. It is the fine flowering of respect and admiration, of mutual understanding and shared goals. It is the normal relationship of mature individuals and can fit—has fitted, as the annals of many Communities show—into the framework of religious obedience.

It might well be that pervading friendship, understood, appreciated, and cultivated in religious Communities, would prove to be the healing agent in the three "ailing" areas here analyzed. Certainly a strong spirit of friendship could help to reconcile existing differences of opinion—and even bewilderment—concerning the practice of corporate and personal poverty. A spirit of true friendship both for special appointees and the beginning members of the Community will dictate deep thought and careful selection of well-educated and specially trained Mistresses at the various levels of counseling. And finally, and in the last analysis most importantly, in the knowledge and confidence of supporting friendship Superiors would find the valor and the promptitude to exercise the kind of *dynamic* leadership called for now. For what could give more sureness, more certainty to the trumpet blast than the knowledge that friend calls to friend!

7

Sisters, Isn't It About Time?

An anti-Pentecostal spirit is upon us. Each of us hears his own tongue spoken by his fellow citizens, and each puts a different interpretation upon the spoken word. No longer do words have an exclusive or definite meaning. This semantic situation is far more disadvantageous to the writer than to the speaker. The latter can correct and clarify his meaning; but for the writer "what is written is written," and readers interpret according to their personal reactions.

•   •   •

This linguistic multi-talk, this use of old terms to express new concepts, is evident in the world of religion today. To narrow the focus, there is among many who speak and write of the religious life much wresting of words from their original meaning. Much of the confusion, anxiety and uncertainty now prevalent among Sisters arises from this use of old terms in new contexts. This unrest would dissolve if, in our constant flow of dialogue, we observed and insisted that others observe the scholastic maxim "Define your terms," to make sure that we all know exactly what we're talking about. Is it not wholly in keeping with the spirit of Christianity to check all definitions and decisions against the teachings and example of Christ?

His was the example, His were the teachings which first determined us to follow—many years ago or few—when we (to use the words of the *Decree on Renewal*) "set about following Christ with greater freedom and imitating Him more closely through the practice of the evangelical counsels." Quite possibly the greatest service we can render the Church, our respective

89

communities and the generation that will come after us will be to help keep religious life on an even keel. Sisters, isn't it about time that each of us, in her own way and according to her opportunities, makes certain that the religious life remains a true and intelligent following of Christ; a going about, as He did, doing good?

Isn't it about time, Sisters, that we stop, listen and evaluate what is being said and written about religious life today, and check it against our own knowledge and experience?

Isn't it about time that we look at our image as projected by communications media today, and ask ourselves if it is a valid one, in which we recognize ourselves, our companions and our superiors as persons made in the image and likeness of God and dedicated to His service?

• • •

Isn't it about time that when we are urged to be "just like laywomen" in their manner of life, mode of dress and accepted social customs, we answer positively and finally: "No, thank you"? After all, we are not asking the laity to be "just like us" —they wouldn't want it, and neither would we.

Isn't it about time that all of us who are working vigorously for the reform and renewal prescribed by the Church speak out clearly so that our voices may be heard? Who has a better right to speak for us than we ourselves?

To get to the heart of the matter: Isn't it about time that we halted the trend toward secularizing the religious life?

SISTERS AND THE SECULAR CITY

Secularism is a harsh term. Or, rather, it *was* a harsh term. But now many writers, popular and prolific, have given the word an air of high respectability and even desirability. . . . For no philosophy of life that has an almost exclusively temporal frame of reference can serve the purpose of a life based on the supernatural and essentially eschatological in its implications. The religious life can never be recast to fit fully into a secular mold.

The argument in favor of attempting this secularization is based on the premise that since the apostolate of Sisters lies in the secular city where they work with and for seculars, they should not present too open and obvious a contrast to them. The argument, specious and simplistic, is but the preliminary step leading to the acceptance of the frequently advanced statement that, since all Christians are called by God to a special, individual holiness, the religious vocation is not something unique, is not a distinct "call" from God, and does not, *per se,* demand a closer imitation of Christ than is expected of the ordinary lay person. How can we reconcile this notion with the clear words of *Lumen Gentium,* which says: "The religious state is not an intermediary one between the clerical and lay states. Rather, the faithful of Christ are called by God from both these latter states of life so that they may enjoy this particular gift in the life of the Church"? These words would seem to establish the fact that the religious state is not necessarily "better" but certainly "different" from both clerical and lay. . . . Isn't it about time, Sisters, that we recognize this secular source of thinking and resolve that all religious must hold to this difference as a fundamental principle?

RENEWAL VS. REDUCTION

"Divide and rule" is a military axiom. Its modern version is "reduce and destroy." It is part of the universal blight of mediocrity, which would reduce everything to the same level. Witness the curious and contradictory fact that those who condemn religious Communities for requiring uniformity of their members cry out against Sisters being *different,* demanding that they conform to the masses.

As I write, I have before me a picture of two Sisters. One is dressed in the traditional habit of her order. The other as an "experiment" is wearing becoming lay attire, her hair nicely coiffured, her shoes suitably tapered and high-heeled. To what purpose? In laying aside her nun's habit, the Sister has ceased to be identified with the 182,000 Sisters in the United States. Her lay dress identifies her with the more than sixty million working women in our country. Wherein lies the gain?

The religious habit *is* important; important enough for Vatican Council II to give directions for the habit to be adopted when Sisters put aside their former archaic dress: "Since the habit constitutes one of the signs of a consecrated life, it should be simple and modest, at once poor and becoming." In urging Sisters to wear lay attire the reductionists aim at destroying not only the sign itself but all for which it stands. The whole matter of there being a "call" to the religious life, whether it constitutes a state different from that of the laity, whether there is a definite, inherent value in vows that bind one to the observance of the evangelical counsels—all this is questioned and even boldly attacked. The questions and attacks can be disturbing, unless calmly and consistently checked against the Church's teachings in the postconciliar documents of Vatican Council II.

Isn't it about time, Sisters, that we earnestly and purposefully read these documents, rather than excerpts and quotations from them? They are eminently readable, concise and to the point, so different from some encyclicals that are indirect and wordy, baffling in their ambiguity. Vatican II documents are clear and unmistakable in their meaning. There and there alone will we find cogent and valid directives that we can trust in our quest for religious growth; there, too, will we find prudent and positive guidelines concerning the choice and exercise of apostolic works.

Sisters, isn't it about time that we reappraised the validity of our various apostolates, not in light of what Cardinal Suenens says (*The Nun in the World* made its own valuable contribution by stirring us to think) but in light of contemporary social developments, and of Pope Paul's words on the needs of the Church? Reappraisal does not mean rejection of the time-honored apostolates of education, health and welfare in which Sisters have served the Church and society for so many centuries. If there is now a probing of our effectiveness in these fields, let us, by all means, join the probers, not oppose them. Let their findings, when valid, be a source of profit to us, not an occasion for defense.

But in doing this, let us not be swayed or impressed by attention-getting headlines; headlines that depend upon a degree of shock for impact. One such headline recently proclaimed: "Nun Says Don't Call Me Nanny!" Then followed a Sister's indignant declaration: "It's time people stopped thinking of nuns as schoolmarms, nursemaids and nannies in the Church." It is almost certain that few Sisters (none of my acquaintance) think of themselves in those categories, but let's look at it anyway. Loosely, the objectionable terms used refer to teachers, nurses and social workers.

Perhaps it would be well to assess first the validity of "schoolmarm" as applied to our teaching sisters, since teaching is the field in which the largest number of Sisters exercise their apostolate in the United States. After all, the term "schoolmarm" is an early American relic of the one-room schoolhouse where, not unlike Mother Hubbard, a poorly prepared teacher had so many classes she hardly knew what to do. But if there are today such schoolmarms among us, rather than creative teachers, these have indeed missed the boat for the greatest opportunity ever offered to make an educational contribution startlingly relevant to today's world.

Let's face it, Sisters. There are indeed some nuns who loudly complain that they are nothing but glorified "baby-sitters" confined to a classroom in which they find no "adult" inspiration. If that is their fixed interpretation of their role in the apostolate of elementary-school teaching, one is moved to the conclusion that the "baby" is at the podium and the "sitters" (God pity them) at the pupils' desks. Shouldn't we admit that in the not-so-recent past there *was* some "keeping school" rather than "teaching school"? But isn't that the exception today? Isn't it time to take a long, calm, cool look at what our parochial schools have achieved—and what they may yet achieve?

THE PARISH SCHOOL APOSTOLATE

Standing out clearly is the fact that the dedication of the teaching Sisters and their firm ability to keep "first things first" made Catholic education relevant both to a growing nation, primitive and pioneer, and to the Church striving for an immigrant foothold in the new and exciting Land of Liberty. Continuing the dedication and zeal of their predecessors, contemporary teaching Sisters with up-to-date professional preparation are sharpening their insights razor-keen, recognizing the new frontiers before them. A crusading ardor is kindled by these words of *Perfectae Caritatis:* "Institutes should promote among their members an adequate knowledge of the social conditions of the times they live in and of the needs of the Church." To what purpose? "That burning with apostolic zeal they should be able to assist men more effectively." The Church has sounded the challenge for involvement in world affairs, and teaching Sisters have a greater and more unique opportunity—as well as a most pressing obligation—to answer the call.

Isn't it time then, Sisters, that we asked ourselves questions of deeper dimensions than how short our skirts should be and whether or not to choose a headdress that will display our hair—curly or straight? For example, isn't it true that we have failed society in some areas of service; that we have been derelict in a most important duty? For those of us whose teaching experience goes back a decade or more, the answer is writ large and clear for all to read in the Declaration of Independence, the Constitution of the United States and the Bill of Rights—all of which we taught with so much pride. But did we really help the students to make these principles a living reality in their daily lives?

For who among us, Sisters, (ten, twenty or thirty years ago) pointed out how sharply and how heavily the burden of inequality bore down upon minority groups, particularly upon the Negro citizens of the United States? Who among us insisted in season and out of season that racial equality, public accommodations, equal job opportunities and open housing were a moral right for all American citizens of a country founded on the principles of freedom and human rights? Let's stand up and be counted— who among us taught these principles with the rigor and dedication that we taught the three Rs? The fourth R falls by default, since teaching tolerance instead of prejudice, brotherly love for men of all cultures, independent of color, race and creed, is of the essence of religion.

How many of us were deterred by sheer indifference, or the diversionary tactic: "Those are political matters and as such have no place in the classroom"? Ah, what a waste of opportunity to serve God and country was there! Most of us have long since tried to atone by our tears and prayer: Forgive us, Lord, for we knew not of what we were robbing both ourselves and our

pupils while there was still time.

COMES A SECOND AND MAIN CHANCE

Now that the white man's injustice and inhumanity to the black man have precipitated a crisis in our country, the Church, through her Priests, Brothers and Sisters, has moved belatedly into action. Religious join in public protests and demonstrations and proudly walk in picket lines. They risk their lives in violent riots where "white power" strives to subdue "black power" and vice versa. Participation in these activities is highly commendable. But don't we often reflect today, Sisters, on how much stronger and farther-reaching our influence would have been had we begun decades ago to bring about social reform through a day-to-day insistence in our classrooms that racial prejudice, hate and intolerance are social sins that simply cannot be tolerated by a correct conscience?

It is tempting to wonder about the guilt feelings we so easily aroused about the Sixth Commandment while completely passing over Our Lord's teachings (and example) concerning the brotherhood of man without reference to racial or ethnic origins. How wonderful it would have been had we used the potent power of "Sister said" to shape the thinking of the parents of our pupils to a point where they saw clearly the rank injustice of rejecting a man because of the color of his skin. Think, Sisters, of what might have been!

Isn't it just, then, that we Sister-teachers feel the all-but-intolerable pangs of guilt over the evidence of our failure to teach divine, or even an honest, human charity? There is abundant testimony of our assent by silence to racial inequities. One of the bitterest race riots of our strife-torn times took place in a city that claims to have one of the best Catholic school systems in the United States. As I read the account of the Chicago race riots, one incident stood out. Sisters (God bless them) were marching with the demonstrators. Suddenly and violently, a rock found its mark on the head of one of the Sisters. It was no accident. The rock was aimed directly and arrived on target, accompanied with the words, "That's for you, Nun." Shocking, yes. Deplorable, yes.

Isn't there a dreadful symbolism here which prompts us to believe that the rock was aimed at all of us in the teaching apostolate, with the words: "That's for *you*, Nun, for not teaching me 'way back in early grade school that it was a sin to hate my black or foreign-born brother. That's for you, Nun, for forming me to be a Catholic parishioner, but not a Christian witness. That's for you, Nun, for not showing me, young as I was, that ballot-box intimidation, rack-rents and enforced unemployment are all forms of legal theft and oppression. That's for you, Nun, for never telling me about the poor, but gearing your teaching, religious and moral, to the middle-class respectability in which I so comfortably lived." Thank you, Sister Angelica, for taking this for us—especially for any Sister today who calls elementary-school teaching a job for baby-sitters. Thank you, Sister Angelica, for marching on, undeterred by the blow, wiping the blood from your face. I am still wiping mine.

Sisters, let's learn from this near-tragic event that the activities we engage in outside the classrooms, in behalf of our neighbor (witnessing Christ in the marketplace) are valid only insofar as they complement the teaching given within our parish schools. We have taught our children to learn; and today we are assisted, not only by a good professional background ourselves, but with the most efficient equipment of all time. But how many times, in how many places, at how many conventions, have we heard (without listening) the complaint that "religion and the social sciences are the weakest areas in our schools"? Yet it is in these subjects that we find the greatest opportunities to teach our children to love.

Now that the Church wishes that the teaching of religion be scripturally based, we will be pretty well embarrassed by some passages, unless we teach universal love. Shall we point out that Catholic families are above average in stability as one evidence of familial love? "If you love those who love you, what credit shall you have? Do not even the publicans do that?" (Matt. 5: 46). Shall we cite our pluralistic society as an almost insurmountable barrier? "There is neither Gentile nor Jew, circumcised nor uncircumcised, Barbarian nor Scythian, bound nor free. But Christ is all and in all" (Col. 3:11).

Shall we defensively argue that the product of Catholic education, according to the latest comprehensive study, has a slight academic edge on those not so educated? Shall we refute charges by insisting that Catholic pupils are not "isolated" from other Americans (the charge is silly, at best) and that they are tolerant of all religions, and—we really ought to italicize this one—that if they attend Catholic colleges they show less prejudice than other Americans, especially toward black people and Jews? Now why should this difference be noted only at the college level, and then only by comparison?

No, Sisters, it is not much to be proud of; it is wholly unworthy of our dedication to teaching, our better-than-average professional preparation, our commitment to the Church, to our community, to our students. Somewhere, some time ago—probably in the not-so-distant past—our thinking was derailed, quite

possibly by howls to the right of us and howls to the left of us
that "teaching is not really an apostolate." In which case, what
becomes of our Catholic schools and the Church's mandate to
teach? Or, for that matter, of the public schools in which thousands of dedicated teachers think of their profession as the
lifestream of our country? We have allowed ourselves to be
ridiculed into believing that elementary schools can be served by
"baby-sitters" and "nannies" while the more "adult" Sister turns
to the social apostolate in the Church—for which, let us add in
all sincerity, the teaching Sister is not prepared professionally,
and in which, unless she takes time out for sound preparation, it
is quite possible she will do more harm than good.

In attempting to build the Great Society, President Johnson
practically and realistically began with education, which places a
huge responsibility upon teachers. Perhaps it is time, Sisters, to
grasp now our second chance to do a better job in the teaching
apostolate with all of its varied ramifications and implications. In
developing the full potential of "our main chance" let us not be
deluded as to the means we have at our disposal to make a
stupendous contribution in building a better world and, I un-
hesitatingly add, a more relevant Church.

Our efforts toward these ends, and the more immediate task
of solving the problems that stand in the way, are not based outside the classrooms of our schools. Rather, they exist within
their framework, and in the minds and hearts of the thirty or
forty pupils who are ours for five hours every day by direct
contact and ours by association for the rest of their lives. Teaching, by its very nature, is preventive—preventing ignorance and
all the evils that derive from it.

"SISTERS SHOULD BE OUT WITH THE PEOPLE"

Sisters, isn't it about time we evaluated this slogan in light of
what the Church actually says in her documents on renewal and
adaptation in the religious life? More and more we hear that
Sisters should make themselves accessible to the people of God.

Yes, a resounding yes, to that. To make this feasible, part of the renewal now taking place in many Communities has dictated a change in rules and regulations, in horaria and customs, in order to bring about a refreshingly updated attitude toward the working together of laity and religious. Teaching CCD classes; participation in diocesan "Little Councils"; visiting parishioners in their homes; attendance at night events, both professional and civic—these are common in many places: so common that whereas such happenings once rated a picture, nuns are now only a name "among those present" in the publicity lists.

But Sisters, let's get it straight. In the ever-louder cry for Sisters to "be human," let us remember that we *are* human, so let's not undertake to work day *and* night, but keep it to day *or* night. Was not the monastic custom of rising to pray at night abolished because it unfitted the Sister for her strenuous day? Isn't it contradictory to now introduce additional sleep-preventing activities because "Sisters should be with the people"? We are human—that's what they want us to be—and, like other humans, we live forever in the looming shadow of frayed nerves, hardened arteries and damaged hearts, all of which take their toll.

THE INSTITUTION-BASED APOSTOLATE

"Going out to the people" is becoming more and more opposed to the work of Sisters in institutions, particularly in hospitals and social agencies. Let's take a long and thoughtful look at our institution-based apostolates. What are they but service stations? Yes, service stations just as surely as department stores, banks and hotels are. As a matter of fact, the more critically one looks at Catholic institutions, the more sense they make. They are service stations to which come those who need what they offer in health and welfare. If the Sisters now engaged in hospitals and social agencies would decide, for the greater glory of God and the good of mankind, to bring their services personally to the people, just how much could they accomplish as measured against what they are now doing? How many persons would they meet? What would be their impact on sickness and suffering, poverty and deprivation in the community they serve as compared with the far-reaching influence they exert in the "service stations" they staff?

Certainly the Sister-nurse and the Sister-social worker should not and happily do not limit their services to institutions. Many Sisters qualify for membership in the Visiting Nurses Association; a still larger number have the practice of following up discharged patients with visits to their homes. An arthritic old man living alone, or a mother with a chronic coronary condition, or any other home situation requiring nursing skills is part of a hospital Sister's apostolate. The Chicago story of the teaching Sisters' success in the urban apostolate is its own proof of what can be accomplished by spending one Saturday each week in the inner city. The trouble about the whole matter lies in our youthful, robust American temperament which expresses its enthusiasm— and demonstrates its fickleness—by the either/or attitude. If the new is good, ergo, the old is bad. Off with its head! But somehow the heads of Sisters are exasperatingly well fixed. Let's keep them that way, Sisters.

Let our thinking be crystal clear. Or, infinitely better, let it reflect the wisdom of the Holy Spirit. We can indeed serve all mankind and in all ways. What we cannot do is serve *two* masters. We have the word of divine authority for that. Any atempt at fusing secularity with religious life generates hostility: "Either he will hate the one and love the other, or he will devote himself to one and despise the other" (Matt. 6:24). Herein lies the difference between Christianity and secularism. Here, too, is the field of the reductionists. Under the most plausible arguments, based on "service," they would have religious women cast off as unnecessary impedimenta all that is supernatural in their professional lives. To this end we are urged to abandon all that distinguishes us from our lay associates. In short, secularists equate a religious vocation with a service career.

The Church thinks quite otherwise. In *Lumen Gentium,* religious are referred to as "signs." In *Perfectae Caritatis,* this is expanded into "blazing emblems of the heavenly kingdom." Are signs to say nothing? Are blazing emblems to have no significance? Isn't it about time, Sisters, that we take ourselves as seriously as the Church takes us and see if we measure up as signs? To be effective, a sign must stand out boldly, be instantly distinguishable, have a constant significance, be accurate in its message and positive in its directions. When the Sister, as a sign, faithfully fulfills all these conditions, she becomes indeed a flaming symbol of the love of Christ and the genuine brotherhood of man.

BUT WHAT OF THE SISTER SHORTAGE?

Yes, Sisters, what about it? There is indeed a rather frantic search going on among the members of religious Communities— and among clergy and laity, too—to fix the blame for the fewness of vocations to the religious life. It is surprising how many of the laity, especially our laywomen (witness the number of letters to the editors of our diocesan papers, to say nothing about Betty South's "Sister Androgyne" in the October issue of *U.S. Catholic*), point to what they call the "senseless experimentation" going on among the various Sisterhoods in parish convents and Catholic colleges. "Experimentation" is just fine—if it is carried on with the prudence recommended by the Church in her decrees and documents dealing with adaptation and renewal. But the "experimentation" now in progress seems to be preoccupied almost entirely with worldly dress and lay living; while the "renewal" seems to concern itself with repossessing what we once renounced by our vow of poverty and obedience.

Small wonder, then, that prospective candidates are confused as to just what constitutes a truly religious vocation. As we all know, the habit is not the monk, but it *is* the sign that makes visible the consecration inherent in a life lived by vow. For just one example, what becomes of poverty (which includes the use of time) if 182,000 religious women become involved in the daily problem of "What shall I wear today? How shall I style my hair?"

These experiments in secularizing the religious life are not calculated to increase vocations among young women who understand the words, "Renounce yourself and come follow Me."

However, ascribing the blame for the vocation shortage to faults within religious communities themselves, to parental opposition, to the indifference of the clergy, to the new breed of young people today can all probably be justified up to a point. But why assume that the reduction in numbers has only a culpable source? Isn't it quite possible that we would take a quite different viewpoint if we analyzed this seeming liability from God's point of view? Let us recall that incident in the Gospel where Christ's disciples, seeing a man born blind, immediately leaped to judgmental conclusions, asking: "Was this man guilty of sin, or was it his parents' [sins] that he should have been born blind?" Christ answered at once: "Neither he nor his parents were guilty; it was so that God's action might declare itself in him" (John 9:2-3). A thoughtful reflection on all of the conditions and circumstances involved in the decrease in vocations may lead to the conviction that this is God's way of manifesting a truth to us, and that His action is not punitive, but rather paternal and protective.

For at this moment in history, the Church is not seeking greater expansion but newer and deeper dimensions in holiness. Religious Communities of women have the same goal. Their attention and efforts, during this transitional era, are not geared so much to an increase in membership as to an emphasis on excellence in God's service. Wherever changes are made there are always accompanying mistakes, given the frailty and fallibility of human nature. The Gospel shows how some refused Christ's call, and others, who were once His ardent disciples, found His words "a hard saying" and walked no more with Him. If today there are fewer admissions and more defections in the religious life, probably neither the Church nor the Communities themselves will really suffer in the long run. This interim affords us time in which to probe the motives of those who apply for entrance, and time in which to evaluate those who leave and those who remain steadfast in their vocation. We need to do both. Just as surely as the end product of multiplying zeroes by zeroes is zero, so mediocrity multiplied by mediocrity results only and always in mediocrity. Isn't it time to face the facts, Sisters, that only excellence is good enough for God?

Nor is it true—as is sometimes alleged by Sisters unclear in their definitions and in their value judgments—that "the best Sisters are leaving." Charity sternly (and rightly) forbids any judgmental attitude toward those who, having once put their hand to the plow, later look back. But those of us living in our respective Communities know that we can say with certainty that "the best Sisters are staying," living out their promises to God. For if we do not joyfully keep our promises to God, to whom will we make promises meant to be kept? Surely it was these "best Sisters" whom Pope Paul had in mind when he said recently:

The Church loves you for the vivid and striking example which, in spite of criticism and aversion, makes you extremely precious to her. If there is still so much good in the world, it is because there are those who look to you . . . and draw from your example the strength to remain faithful amidst difficulties and temptations.
Address to Nuns, Rome. May 16, 1966

Yes, indeed, the best Sisters are staying; staying amidst storms, knowing that in God's good time the commanding "Peace, be still" will be heard throughout the land. These "best Sisters" are standing valiantly by the Church, remaking many of the externals of their lives according to her directives and seeking constantly to deepen their religious dedication. These best Sisters are using their intelligence and intellectual energy to cultivate newer and more sharply defined attitudes toward the assumption of personal responsibility which will enable them to measure more accurately and tread more courageously the newer paths opening to them.

These thousands of valiant religious will soon be a beacon to the numberless candidates now adopting a wait-and-see period while probing their own motivation. Likewise, they will be a steadying and stabilizing influence among all the religious women who valiantly strive to be what the Church wants and needs today: neither "new nuns" nor, for that matter, "nuns of the future," but *renewed* Sisters; renewed in Christ Jesus, today, tomorrow and forever.

8

Fire, Flood, Earthquake—
Sursum Corda, Sisters!

History is the record of man's reaction to disaster, personal and cosmic. Almost invariably he uses catastrophe as a catalyzing agent to rebuild on that which nature has destroyed. Narrowing instances to our own country, let us recall the overwhelming destruction caused by the Chicago fire, the Galveston flood, the San Francisco earthquake. After the first brief period of disorientation, anguish, and helplessness, the spirit of man dominated the destruction of nature. Brought closer together by the very forces that had momentarily separated and disrupted them, the citizenry closed ranks and in a spirit of fraternal unity and fortitude attacked their common problems. The result in each case was a greater and grander city, one planned to better meet contemporary needs on every level; a city functionally designed around the parts undestroyed by the disaster to serve its citizens more effectively and profitably.

THE CHURCH TODAY

The Catholic Church today is not unlike a city that has been violently shaken to its very foundations. The soft, fresh breeze of Pope John's open window has whipped up to hurricane proportions, and the spirit of man is responding. Much that was once held sacred and untouchable is now being discarded or modified past the point of recognition. Much that was once considered essential and unchangeable is now being abolished.

Persons closest to the heart of a fire, the force of a flood, the center of an earthquake are first and most fully affected by its

105

violence. It follows, then, that those whose entire lives are devoted to the Church—the bishops, priests and religious—should feel most deeply the vibrations of the winds that have so profoundly shaken her. These, too, are the very persons who, by reason of their charisma of consecration and dedication, will enter with eager hope and zest into the replanning and renewing of the City of God, so that we can serve the City of Man more effectively. But we cannot do it alone; and not necessarily as leaders. For one of the most constructive effects of Vatican II is the Jericho-like destruction of the wall of separation between bishops and priests, clergy and laity, laity and religious. Now the People of God are reaching out hands to one another, realizing, like citizens in a disaster area, that "we are all in this thing together" so let's get on with the job of creative repair.

More and more class barriers are down and indigenous leadership sought and accepted when offered in a spirit of good will. Even as the present day Chicago, Galveston, and San Francisco reckon their growth, expansion, and prosperity from the catastrophe that forced their citizens to rethink, replan, and rebuild, uniting all minds and hearts in the process, so will the Church look back to this post-conciliar era as the moment in history when, discarding accretions in liturgical practice and the impedimenta that have accrued to religious life, its soul went marching on. For the Church must and will keep marching on; and only if the Church keeps marching will the religious life be in step with the times. This is what we are all working for now—even before we have seen the end of fire, floods, and quakes.

FORMALISM—THE ENEMY WITHIN

The breakdown of barriers between bishops, clergy, religious, and laity is only one of the pluses resulting from the wholesale shaking up of the Church. Formalism, long enthroned as a lesser god, entrenched as an untouchable power, had vitiated and even turned from their authentic purpose many customs, practices, and traditions of the Church in its organizational, administrative, and liturgical functions. When the post-conciliar upheaval dislodged these accretions and impedimenta and caused them to totter, crumble and, in some instances, to disappear, nowhere was the effect felt more alarmingly than in religious communities. For here indeed was a breeding place for formalism; and here had blindly accepted customs carried formalism to the undeserved dignity of authentic tradition. In light of what the renewal era is revealing, one would say that most of the panic, and much of the pain and perplexity that have swept through the ranks of religious women in the last few years, were induced in one way or another by having to deal effectively with formalism.

FORMALISM AN ATTITUDE OF MIND

Formalism may be described as an attitude of mind that habitually attaches more importance to the exterior than to the interior, to the form of an action rather than its meaning. It places greater emphasis on the *way* a thing is done than on the *why* it should be done. Formalism focuses on the *plan* rather than on the *purpose;* it centers on method rather than on motivation. Rigidity is its outstanding "virtue" and exactitude is its safeguard. Its values are quantitative rather than qualitative; and because its effects are so opposite to those apparently aimed at, one may almost apply to formalism the self-contradictory term, *materialistic spirituality*.

Because attitude dictates action, formalism can permeate and even vitiate every area of a Sister's personal life and, one might say, of community life in general. A thoughtful analysis of the criticisms of the religious life—those that come from within, beginning with the Church—is directed to those customs and traditions that betray the unwholesome influence of formalism. Formalism can be found everywhere—in the governmental and organizational structure, in the regulations that concern the apostolate, the interpretation of the vows, the prayer life, both corporate and personal, in the attitude toward penance and self-denial, and in the exercise of corporate and personal fraternal charity and justice.

If not actually written into the Constitution and Rule, traditionalism has all too often sanctioned if not *dictated* formalism in their execution. Small wonder, then, that newly received as well as older Sisters who have lived the religious life valiantly, loving and cherishing it, now cry out against what formalism is so apt at doing—equating trivia with all that is substantial and of vital significance. "You tithe mint and anise and cummin, and have left undone the weightier matters of the law, right judgment and mercy and faith" (Matt. 23:23). Well indeed has the decree on renewal been titled *Perfectae Caritatis!*

FORMALISM IN PRAYER LIFE

In accordance with the spirit and the specific wording of *Perfectae Caritatis,* all changes in Constitution and Rule, organizational and structural, are to be viewed as a means to one great end: the individual renewal of each Sister. For most certainly if each member of every religious Community is genuinely renewed in spirit and in truth, as the Council calls for, then the whole religious life will be renewed in spiritual and physical vigor. A close examination of three areas of our lives will show us clearly how formalism militates against this individual renewal the Church is seeking for her religious women.

Each Community, lawfully and necessarily, has always had its common or corporate form of prayer. Essentially this includes the holy sacrifice of the Mass, the whole or parts of the Office, meditation, particular examen, and spiritual reading. To these essentials, most communities add (in private or common) the rosary, the Stations of the Cross, novenas, litanies, and other lengthy devotions unique and dear to the heart of each community. Thus even Mary, seated at the feet of Jesus, is busy about many things.

In this context, prayer took on a kind of endurance test; it became a veritable marathon where survival became a test of fitness. Small wonder, then, that prayer became, to many Sisters, something of a burden rather than a daily and permanent joy, and too often spirituality was reduced to statistics It is hard to see here any relation to Christ's promise that his yoke would be sweet and his burden light.

Yet we know that yoke can provide a sense of guidance, and

a burden not too heavy can give a feeling of purpose. It is not surprising then, that when Community prayers were revised and shortened, when the Church's liturgy took precedence over communal devotions, many Sisters felt a sense of uncertainty amounting almost to shock. In the instances where piety was real, although nourished on rigidity and exactitude, Sisters came through the ordeal of crucial change firm and fast in their devotedness to their respective Communities and to their religious vocation. But where formalism produced a brittle, shallow piety, there was a withering away for lack of roots that nourished. Sadder yet, where formalism was not recognized for the foe of religious life that it is, and where no major changes were made, there was a complete or partial turning from it, to find a richer and more Christ-like soil.

FORMALISM IN CONSTITUTION, RULES AND CUSTOMS

No lesser authority than that of the Holy See could have brought about the thorough and critical revision of constitutions, rules, and customs, begun some years ago by many Communities and continuing as an ongoing process today. What the repeated urgings of Pope Pius XII failed substantially to effect, the Decrees of Vatican II are accomplishing. The Motu Proprio *Ecclesiae Sanctae* prescribes a time limit of 1968 for the convening of General Assemblies to effect recommended revisions—to put the stamp of approval on changes already made or in an experimental stage, and to open the way for further adaptations.

UNIFORMITY VS. UNITY

In the process of putting into determined effect the Church's directive to "adapt their manner of living, praying and working" to contemporary "physical and psychological conditions," uniformity, that omnipresent bastion of formalism, was the first to fall. Too long had religious Communities boasted of the merits of uniformity, both as a means and as an end. Even those congregations given to multiple works had identical regulations covering rising and retiring, work and prayer, meals and recreation.

In the new light now given them by Vatican II, Sisters see clearly that this exact uniformity, far from contributing to union —that union prayed for by Christ "that they may be one, Father, as you and I are one"—actually militated against the very ideal they sought. Many times uniformity was maintained only at the cost of greater tension, disruption of interpersonal relationships, and a limitation of apostolic zeal. Uniformity, solid and rigid, is inherently opposed to the strength and flexibility of unity, which, like God, always surrounds itself with and rejoices in variety. The very word uni-form, meaning that it has but one form, is the antithesis of union, which is the harmonious blending of a number of elements. Given the large liberty of the decree *Perfectae Caritatis,* all but a very few Communities have, for the most part, initiated changes—changes aimed at freeing the life-giving spirit from the deadening weight of the letter.

AUTHORITY WITH EQUALITY FOR ALL

Let us take one example: authority—that hardy perennial whipping boy of today's critics. With the Council's definition of authority as "service" the whole climate of religious authority changed. Such titles as "Mother" or "Venerable Mother" are being successively dropped by an increasing number of Communities in favor of "Sister" as an all-encompassing term. This simple act is freighted with significance. It not only abolishes the idea of maternalism, but it sets status where it belongs. It indicates a permeating spirit of collegiality and makes for greater ease in establishing the now attainable goal of subsidiarity. It implies full recognition that all members of a community are equal, and that all members of the Community have the same, identical claim upon it. After all, each of us bought membership with the same price—our whole life, our all. As we learn from Christ's praise of the widow's mite, it is not the amount given but the "all-ness" that constitutes the purchasing power. With this recognition of the basic equality of all members, certain practices and rules not in conformity with it are being dropped or drastically revised.

In the assembling and mingling of Sisters for Community

purposes today, neither position nor seniority are the invariable arbiters of where each Sister shall sit, when she shall speak and— more important—what she shall say. This deemphasizing of rank has proven a valuable factor in bringing the easy informality of group living into the lives of Sisters, with accruing benefits— social, intellectual, and spiritual.

The illogical practice dictated by undiluted formalism, of making no provision in rules, customs, social life, and spiritual practices for the proven, experienced Sister over the neophyte, is coming to be recognized as a policy that is as detrimental to the religious life as it would be to the professional. This is not to impugn the equality of youth with age. It is rather to recognize that youth needs solid scaffolding to enable it to build its edifice of religious character; but how incongruous to retain scaffolding once the building is erected and can stand alone!

As a matter of truth, those of us who were born into our respective Communities and bred under these policies experienced no trauma; it exercised little influence *de facto,* or we would not have today the numerous cadres of Sisters in the educational, health, social, and missionary fields. But since, *de jure,* no differentiation was made, some Sisters—a minority to be sure— fashioned their lives by the letter-of-the-law mentality, converting routine (once it had done all it could for them) into ritualism, and exactitude into excellence. The net result was a sturdy mediocrity and a stultifying waste.

In a way, these literal-minded Sisters were sinned against. The Decrees of renewal recognize this and are urging much-needed changes in rules and practices to make liberal allowance for a Sister's individual responsibility. . . .

Some Sisters will say, "But *I* have not seen these changes— we still do what we always did before!" To this I can only whisper, "Patience! The year 1968 will see wonders, once all the chapters begin to swing." (But whisper it only in the garden— and over the garden hedge.) This reminds me: *secrecy,* that bane of all that is good and holy and charitable, is on the way out. Collegiality will take care of that. (Go tell it on the mountain.)

• • •

In actual practice, the net result of reevaluation leaves Sisters free for the larger things of their vocation. Time formerly spent on Community minutiae is so much time saved for larger thinking on major contemporary matters. When all essential changes have been accepted, the revised rules and customs will go far toward restoring all things in Christ. For the odd thing about adaptation and renewal is that, when truly achieved, they will not make religious life easier or more comfortable, or free any of us from the necessity of daily self-denial; but with the revision of rule and custom self-denial will become a truly positive virtue, and self-sacrifice will still be the bulwark of our dedication.

But renewal won't really make Sisters new or modern or even precisely contemporary. What it will do, if we cooperate with grace, will be to restore the religious life to its original Christian simplicity. Then indeed will we be Christ-like, remembering the delight He took in His Father's lavish bounty: the birds of the air, the lilies of the field. How He must have drunk in their fragrance as He walked the vales of Galilee, and how He loved the birds, promising them his personal protection. It is formalism —not Christianity—that makes a virtue out of the refusal to enjoy all that the good earth offers, and arouses guilt feelings about appreciating the gladness of the sunshine, the mystery of moonlight and stars, and the significant sounds of cities in action.

FORMALISM IN THE APOSTOLATE

Quite possibly there would not be today the hue and cry against "institutionalism" (one would really like to have its syndrome spelled out) had Sisters not allowed formalism to weigh heavily on their devotedness and impede their efficiency. Where the spiritual, intellectual, and apostolic should have been integrated, formalism dictated that they be compartmentalized. Strict observance "according to the rule" fragmented a Sister's day, and conventual customs were often real barriers to the free functioning of the apostolate. Since the greatest number of Sisters in the United States is found in the field of education, for examples of formalism one turns first to teaching Sisters. Let's frankly admit that parents and pupils suffered, in all too many instances, from our attempts at practicing "religious decorum" (to say nothing of our efforts to personify Stern Duty as the Voice of God). The spontaneity of smile and word was checked. . . . There was no attempt to give off the warmth of love and the sparkle of joy-in-the-world-about-us; formalism kept us "distant" and we disciplined through fear.

Happily, it is the rare child who is not blessed with resiliency, and the merry memories "of fifth grade days with dear old Sister Scholastica"—who, it was whispered, was "strict because she was a saint"—became the hilarious anecdotes later, with small hint of repressive resentment. One can safely say that the children were less scarred than many of their teachers. Telling evidence of this is found in the fact that most of the vocations to our Catholic Sisterhoods come from the schools.

With parents, the story is graver and different. As the convent schedule gave no thought to the parents' work and leisure time, contact with the Sisters to discuss school policies and their children's progress was unusual—and most formal. Appointments of a social nature were as rare as the whooping crane, and until *aggiornamento* changed the rule of never visiting in the children's homes, visits to a child's family were restricted to times of death and disaster. Formalism managed to make this attitude toward home and school relationships seem suitable. As a consequence, even in our post-conciliar era, some schools retain complete autonomy, while parents' responsibility for education of their childrden moves closer and closer to zero.

Actually, the Sisters didn't want things this way—their hearts were not in this rigid social system. Proof of that is seen in their readiness to participate in the new spirit that welcomes not only lay teachers on the school faculty but the volunteer help of mothers in the classroom, the school office, the cafeteria, and the play-yard. Once the democratic process was evidenced in Community government, Sisters readily extended it to all areas of their apostolate.

Sisters working in the health and social welfare fields felt equally with their teaching compatriots the hampering grasp of formalism. As their professional skills attained higher levels, many were looked to for leadership. But where attendance at night meetings was taboo, travel was restricted, a companion was required, decision on some simple matter had to be deferred until "I consult my superior"—the exercise of leadership was inhibited. In these formal circumstances the leadership which a Sister's vocation should foster, and which the Church and society so much need, had little chance to grow. True, there are today a not inconsiderable number of Sisters who are national leaders in their respective fields. This should not give us too much comfort; it only points up how their number could have been multiplied in a less limiting climate.

LET'S STOP CHEATING

By-products are sometimes even more valuable than the original product or goal. It is now evident that the close inter-personal relationships between religious and laity, as a by-product of their original specific services, may well be, in terms of witnessing, of more worth than the services themselves. But there are difficulties too. To narrow this matter to one point in particular, what view should Sisters take, what guidelines should they use, in adopting the frequently and vehemently urged "meaningful relationships" in working closely with laymen, priests, Brothers, seminarians and others of the opposite gender? I always feel that the articulate proponents of "love in spite of the risk involved" protest too much. Younger members of our congregations (men and women both) are asking blunt questions: "How far may we go in this business of friendly involvement?" The answer should be equally blunt. They want to know; they want to hear the answers from those to whom they are answerable in the formative years, and above all they would be glad to hear the answer from those who insist upon its values to personality. But just as children squirm about asking their parents for the facts of life, while the parents often shy away from clear answers, so our young religious question their elders, only to be countered with other questions. Many times they never do get an answer. They should be answered; they should be told the facts of religious life—and if they are not, we may reasonably expect trouble. . . .

Young religious of today's generation go to the heart of the matter. They know when they are being cheated. And cheating is to imbue them with the urge for "meaningful relations" with priests, Brothers, seminarians, and laymen, with no reference to the intrinsic dangers or tragic results—on the increase today because most of us are running scared in terror of being called "old-fashioned." Of course Sisters, priests, seminarians, and Brothers in the altered circumstances of today must work closely, daily and even hourly together. But let's be honest with them; let's tell them of the danger that we instinctively know lurks there and must be reckoned with.

Any person who has the confidence of young Sisters knows how anxiously they say, "I want to exercise universal love, not only with my clients but also with my colleagues—but how far can I go in a spirit of prudence without seeming mistrustful of Brother X or Father Y? For a while I was uncomfortable with both of them, but now I'm afraid I am too comfortable." Looking squarely into the heat and light of the branding iron labeled "old-fashioned," I am going to answer that question. It is simple and direct, though some will say it is simplistic. To the question, "How far can I go?" I would answer forthrightly: "You can be just as friendly and involved in your apostolate as you would wish your mother to be in her parish apostolate. Anything that would be unseemly in her conduct with any priest or layman, would be quite unseemly in yours. If you don't want her to flirt, or to give too lingering a handshake to a man other than your father, or to meet clandestinely, know then that it would be far more unseemly in you, a young religious who has dedicated (or is planning to dedicate) herself entirely to God." This lays it firmly on the line, weighing it not in the balance of the sanctuary but in the ordinary scales universally accepted in the marts of men.

SURSUM CORDA, SISTERS!

History is the eternal teacher. The present upheaval in the

Church, unique in origin, is not a new experience. Each time the resultant good far outweighed the threatened harm. The fires of persecution in the first centuries purified her members. The recurring floods of heresy clarified her doctrines. The earthquake of the Reformation produced an active counter-reformation, though the Church was profoundly shaken to its foundations. Always she emerged from each catastrophe renewed, strengthened, confirmed in her God-given mission. Those who remained faithful during the Church's time of stress shared amply in her restored vigor and vibrancy.

So will it be with the religious life and with those who have persevered while the fires of distorted thinking raged, the floods of disunity beat down the spirit, and the earth shook with searching doubt. The cities of Chicago, Galveston, and San Francisco owe their progress and present proud position to the catastrophes that, by the very havoc they wrought, confirmed the faith of their people in themselves and in their cities.

Let us lift up our hearts, Sisters. Let us shout canticles of joy and confidence. We, dwellers in the City of God while serving the City of Man, will have no lesser experience. If there is no result other than the expulsion of formalism from our lives, giving us a more authentic spirituality with deeper dimensions of dedication, all the fire, floods, and upheavals will have been well worth all we suffered.

Welded together now in the common love of our sublime vocation, in its purification, and with the bonds of fraternal and universal charity strengthened, we have succeeded in doing more than we dreamed—and we will do more. Steadfastly we stood with the Church where she stood. Resolutely we followed when she advanced. Now we will see the promise of a new Jerusalem fulfilled. Humbly singing the Canticle especially reserved to us, renewed Sisters will taste the joy of a new heaven and a new earth.

9

Good-bye, Sister Zoe

Last week Sister Zoe Bossle (two syllables) died. I was astounded to hear that she was eighty-nine years old. I never thought of age in connection with Sister Zoe. I don't remember ever having wondered about it. Sister Zoe never reminded one of age; you were younger when you were in her company because she always radiated youth—at least to me. I was very young when I met Sister Zoe. I remember the event so well because I had just been clothed with the Holy Habit and was setting out on my first mission with my very first Sister Servant (local Superior), who was traveling with me from St. Louis to Louisiana.

We had several adventures on the train—things happen to me—and when we landed early on a Friday morning, Sister Zoe (with *her* Sister Servant) was waiting to greet us. Sister Zoe's smile was like a huge sunflower, and she, like the sunflower, seemed always turned to the sun. She had two outstanding gifts, both of them designed and destined to make others happy. She was a musician. She played the piano like something out of Heaven, and she used it to create joy around her. Her other gift was laughter, and again it was a gift she used for others.

For six years I saw Sister Zoe about every week or two, as I was taking Saturday classes at Loyola University and stayed at St. Theresa School where she was on mission. At one time it had been *St. Simeon Select School for Young Ladies*—these types of "private schools" abounded in the pre-world-war South. But as the years wore on, the neighborhood deteriorated, until it became what we call today an "inner city" school, and as Sister Zoe had served St. Simeon's "young ladies" as music teacher, so later—when it became St. Theresa School—she managed to make the music periods the happiest of the day.

117

Then I was missioned "up North" and the next time I met Sister Zoe was in Texas—some thirty years later. Sister Zoe had turned her everything into pure gold for the Mexicans who attended school at St. Ann's in Dallas. She took great delight in having her pupils give me a taste of their wonderful culture in art, music, and song. How I reveled in their folk music and dances, and their beautiful authentic costumes. It never occurred to me, as I watched Sister Zoe enjoy her beautiful dark-eyed boys and girls, that she had added a year—or thirty—to her lifetime. One simply did not think of age in connection with Sister Zoe.

The next time I had a real visit with Sister Zoe was a year ago at St. Anne's, our residence for senior Sisters. She was in a wheel chair. She scurried around in it like a blue-tail fly, visiting the sick, making fun for her companions, some older, some younger, and *still* I never wondered how old Sister Zoe was. Even arthritis had not lined her face nor dulled her laughter. People took her unfailing good humor for granted—nobody had ever seen Sister Zoe out of sorts.

I never gave that a second thought until last week when the *Ladies Home Journal* came out with an article about Sisters who leave their convents. The man who wrote it—Heaven knows why he chose or was given the subject—is an ex-seminarian, twice divorced, and knows absolutely nothing about Sisters. It was a most unscholarly paper, completely undocumented. For exaggerated statements as to why and how many Sisters left, he could refer only to "responsible sources" and "persons who know"—but he named none of the persons and none of the sources.

But one statement struck me hard. The author (Robert Kaiser, who sometimes writes for *Time* magazine) said that he had interviewed one young Sister—among a dozen—who gave this as her reason: "When I first entered the convent, I was very happy for about ten years. Then suddenly one day I looked at an older Sister, and I saw how bitter she was and I wondered if I'd grow old like that." Presumably she thought she would because, according to her story, she left in fear and trembling that she would grow bitter as the years went by.

Now why? It set me thinking about Sister Zoe because she died the day after I read the *Journal* article. I thought of her gift of laughter which had brought joy to all she met. I thought of her eighty-nine years spent in loving service of God and those around her. And from thinking about Sister Zoe I began to think of all our Senior Sisters at St. Ann's and those right here in the Provincial House Infirmary. I live with them day in and day out. It came to me with a start that in fifty years of Community living, I had never seen one bitter old Sister. Their unselfishness, their cheerfulness, their wonderful spirit of camaraderie is simply a joy to witness. There is Sister Alexis, who will soon be eighty-one years a Sister and ninety-eight years old. She is very alert, still smiling, ready for a word on any of the major issues of the day— and her memory for history and dates is something marvelous. There are Sister Cecilia and Sister Aurea, who have a smile and a wave—and a piece of good news for whoever passes their room. There is Sister Sylvia with her proverbial jokes and twice-told tales, as interesting today as when I entered the Community so many long years ago. You never wonder about her age more than one ever wondered about Sister Zoe Bossle's age. They are just here, making earth a better place to live in with their perennial sparkle and wave of the hand. How can ANYbody ever say that Sisters grow discontented as they grow old? I think it is a sin and a shame to say so.

Good-bye, Sister Zoe, it was such fun knowing you, and such a surprise to think of "eighty-nine" because you always seemed so young, because you had that wonderful gift of laughter that made everybody feel so much at home with you. I blush, remembering that I treated you as a "pal" when I was not yet eighteen, never dreaming you were nearly more than twice-and-a-half my age at that time. But we shall meet again. I'll hear you laughing when I arrive at the pearly gates—then how can I be serious at judgment, knowing you wait just beyond?

10

Raise Your Voice—Cast Your Vote

*An Address delivered before the Chicago Province of
the Adrian Dominican Nuns of Michigan,
May 27, 1967*

The root of democracy is the voice of the people. The fruit
of democracy is the vote of the people. Voice and vote are the
foundations upon which the democratic process rests. Emerging
nations, overturning or disdaining monarchy, reject dictatorship,
sometimes with great violence. All seek for some form of democracy.

The Church, sensitive to the world it serves, is stressing more
and more emphatically those democratic principles, long disre-
garded, but inherent in its organization from the beginning. Thus
society is becoming familiar with the workings of collegiality
among the clergy, and policy-making participated in among the
laity. But for all that has been written about "unrest," "question-
ing," and even "rebellion," in the ranks of religious women, the
very obvious—and hopeful—cause of that restless climate has
largely been overlooked. Today, the Church is continuously
urging religious Communities of women to a more democratic
way of policy-making, always inherent in the constitution, but
never fully expressed or used. This continuous urging of the
Church to Sisters that they now use their voice intelligently and
forcefully is directed toward achieving a better and more decisive
use of their vote in Community affairs.

In steadily increasing numbers, Sisters are becoming keenly
aware that their call to the religious life is making new demands
upon them. These demands are not only in the fields of the
apostolate, but in the less familiar areas of government and

choice. Meeting these demands is part of the price they pay for living more fully a religious vocation in this post-Vatican II era.

For Sisters have now, to a degree mandated by the Church, both a voice and a vote in the day-to-day affairs of their Community. The future of religious life in general and of each congregation in particular, depends upon the courage and intelligence with which each Sister exercises her right of participation in government and her responsibility in freedom of choice. More than that, the whole matter of the renewal of religious life depends upon her use of her voice and vote, since the Decree on Religious Life tells us that "Successful renewal and proper adaptation cannot be achieved unless every member of a Community cooperates."

There is no denying that up to the very recent past, Sisters have been conditioned to stand and wait, believing that they served best when they waited with patience for some change to evolve from circumstances unaided by the group. When a change did happen, whether desired or unwanted, it was seen as "Providence in action." This statement is made by way of explanation, not of condemnation. It is an explanation of why Sisters—possibly the majority—are reluctant to abandon a policy that served so well in the past. It is an explanation, too, of why a minority of the once fully accepting group has finally, openly and almost violently, repudiated the former policy and are so much in the public eye today.

Their rebellion opened the way for the designation of two camps, the "die-hards" (who resist change) and the "far-outs" (who, finding change a heady draught, want more and more of the same). Both the die-hards and the far-outs desire—and desire even passionately—what they deem best for the religious life and for religious women. Neither will reach their goals while each insists on the primacy of *individual interpretation* of what the Church is so plainly asking in the way of renewal and adaptation; and neither will reach their goals until there is honest mutual respect and charity. Has not the decree on renewal been given the significant title of *Perfectae Caritatis?* This difference of opinion is nothing new among those who wish to bear witness to Christ. Paul, when striving to settle dissensions and divisions among the Corinthians gives us the supreme antidote when he says, "Whether Paul or Apollo or Cephas . . . all things are yours, and you are Christ's and Christ is God's" (I Cor. 3:22-23). And even yet, ecumenism has still to resolve the battle of private interpretation of the Scriptures, and the infallibility of the Pope and his collegial aides.

• • •

The first of these groups has been intensely vocal within Communities; the second has been vocal outside of them. It is now time that we heard from the salt-of-the-earth majority group; it is time for them to raise their voices both within and without. They can do this without in any way impugning either the integrity or the intelligence of the others, and with no breach of charity. Charity consists in service; but it is now abundantly clear that the "moderates" can no longer serve if they only wait for order to be restored. They must help to restore it.

Sisters everywhere who are interpreting the intentions of the Church in light of what her leaders have said both in the documents and comments on the *Decree on Renewal* should relinquish the safe but passive role of deploring the downgrading and secularizing of the religious life and assume an active role in upgrading and purifying it from those who seek to de-supernaturalize it. When Christ warned against hiding one's light, He made no reference to the degree of brilliancy it could emanate. He said clearly that it was to be placed upon a candlestick and made plainly visible to all. Now that there is such extensive intra and intercommunity dialogue and discussion, Sisters have an excellent and almost every day opportunity to make known their views and opinions to other Sisters. They should speak out without fear of being branded old-fashioned or not "in the know" or of the in-group. This is a private forum which will ultimately have its effect, a lasting, not a passing effect, on the public forum.

For the present, it would seem wise to think less of the public forum—even if we did not know from experience how ephemeral is its attention, how hollow its impact—and concentrate on the private forum whose strict attention is ever with us. This forum is made up of the companions with whom we live, the persons whom we serve, and all of the laity whose lives touch ours in so many ways. In this forum let us prepare ourselves to be informed, confident spokesmen for the majority view.

To do this, sentiments of devotion and loyalty alone do not suffice. Rather, each Sister should be prepared to speak with authority—and without fear—on what the Church asks of Sisters today. The key to a calm, self-possessed, persuasive leadership is found in a thorough knowledge of the Decrees of Vatican II, especially *The Dogmatic Constitution on the Church,* and *The Pastoral Constitution of the Church in the Modern World, The Decree on Renewal of the Religious Life;* and the Motu Proprio on its implementation should be as familiar to every Sister as is her Holy Office. This, not only because of their intrinsic merit and extensive application to a Sister's life today, but because, like the Scriptures, they can be quoted out of context to support almost any position.

This has indeed been done, and it seems that we are living, to some extent, in an era of "false Christs and false prophets." To combat these the Church has spoken through the present Sovereign Pontiff. We Sisters shall be showing, not negative passivity but positive prudence and religious intelligence by listening to his voice and following his directions. Yet, the interpretation of these directions calls for our discernment as well as our docility; for our understanding as well as our good will.

For, as we have seen, let us admit it, through a want of discernment and understanding, Renewal got off to a misleading start. The Decree stated plainly that both adaptation and renewal were to begin with the individual Sister and only when she was thoroughly renovated in spirit and in truth was it to spread to the larger areas of religious life in general. But what happened? Before individual internal changes could be made, which would result in a deepening of the Sister's prayer life, her more precise interpretation of the Vows, a more thorough knowledge of the Scriptures, a clearer understanding of the role of religious women in the Church and similar vital matters, certain exterior changes were hastily made. These changes, precisely because they were external, immediately caught the attention of the public, Catholic and lay, and because of this, the Sisters, all too often, mistaking the accidentals for the essentials, gave them a disproportionate importance. The external matters which the Sisters too soon stressed and the public seized on so avidly were the extreme modernization of the religious habit, the easier and almost too freely mingling of religious and laity often at improper times. . . . These were not renewal itself, but the appendages of renewal. They were intended by the Church as "experiments" to be tried after the personal renovation of each Sister, and to be judged later as to how far they contributed to the "fundamental norm of the religious life, a closer following of Christ as proposed by the Gospel."

Given the lack of the personal preparation asked for by the Church, perhaps it was to be expected that experimentation would—as it did—soon get out of hand. Despite the fact that the Motu Proprio for implementing the *Decree on Renewal* authorized changes in constitutions and rules on an experimental basis "as long as the purpose, nature and characteristics of the Institute are preserved," some of the experiments seem aimed at the very destruction of those things which they purported to promote and preserve. With growing momentum—not so much in number of Sisters or Communities concerned, as in the noisy publicity engendered by the minority groups—religious habits (even some of those appropriately modernized) were now discarded in favor of lay attire; homey cottages or apartments for small groups replaced convents; and the office of local superior was abolished. "Do mature women need to obey?" Thus disappeared the need for a vow of obedience. Taking paying jobs was highly advocated and practiced. With Sisters thus handling their finances individually, the practice or vow of poverty began to sound as quaint as the *Canterbury Tales*. With "meaningful relationships between the sexes" urged as a requirement for a healthy personality, the safeguards of chastity began to seem as outdated as antimacassars, hence why a vow of virginity?

Once renewal (sic) had gone that far, experimentation rapidly outdistanced the prudence recommended by the Church. Partaking, in public, of cocktails and other alcoholic beverages became more and more a part of accepted social customs; casual attendance at night movies in local theaters seemed "more adult" than going with a group of Sisters at a special matinee; and unless one wishes to look "utterly ridiculous" in lay attire, it had to be supplemented with the use of cosmetics, and a weekly session at a beauty parlor for hair tinting and styling.

In defense of this last, some Sisters say, "I spend no more time at the hairdresser than I formerly spent in starching and shaping the headbands we used to wear." Taking the statement at its face value, one may logically ask, "Where then is the gain? Where is the time and energy *saved?*" The thought back of the modernized religious habit, "simple, modest, hygienic, becoming" was to relieve Sisters of the arduous "starching and wimpling" in order that they might have more time for their apostolic and professional duties. No one will gainsay the fact that there *could* be an apostolate carried on in a beauty parlor— but it does seem as though the hair dryer just might get in the way.

Small wonder that Pope Paul VI found it necessary in addressing the Mothers General at their recent meeting in Rome, to state flatly that, in some instances there had been an excess of "worldliness" in the permitted experimentation. Even this possible excess had been foreseen by Rome and a means to halt it had been prudently provided. The Church has seen little change in human nature over the nearly two thousand years of her existence. A definite time limit has been placed on experimentation: "These experiments may be carried on until the next ordinary chapter, which will have the power to extend them, but not beyond the chapter immediately following." With intuitive prudence, the Holy See has provided that every community must convene a general chapter not later than 1968. In order that the voice of the majority may be heard, and that the majority voice may be implemented by a vote, Rome directs:

In preparing for the chapter, the general council should make suitable provisions for free and extensive consultation of the members, and should correlate the results of this consultation in a way that will help and guide the chapter in its work. It can do this by consulting conventual and provincial chapters, by establishing commissions, by proposing series of question, etc.

Motu Proprio Implementing *Decree on Renewal*

Unheralded by the press, unprogrammed by TV, an irresistible force is now animating religious Communities for women. There are few indeed, young, middle-aged or old, who do not feel a keen sense of personal responsibility to their respective Communities. They are examining, analyzing, assaying their constitutions, rules and customs, their way of life. They realize that before any and every change is proposed, approved and accepted, each Sister has the solemn duty of asking herself, "Will this proposal bring me and my Community closer to Christ? Will it enable us to live more in conformity with His teachings and example as found in the Gospel?"

This is the time, the crucial time, for the vast majority of Sisters who thoroughly believe in the religious life, in the preservation, improvement, and promotion of that life in accordance with the norms given by Vatican Council II, to stand up and be counted. Someone has well said that for evil to triumph it suffices that good men do nothing. The voice of every Sister who resents and resists the attempted de-supernaturalization and the laicization of the religious life must be raised now. The voice of every Sister who believes that the Holy Spirit speaks to her through the Church and our Sovereign Pontiff must be heard in attestation of that faith. The voice of every Sister who accepts the post-conciliar statement that "loyal recognition and safekeeping should be accorded to the spirit of founders, as also to the particular goals and wholesome traditions which constitute the heritage of each community," should sound out loud and clear affirming her agreement. Those who do this now, constantly and conscientiously, in the private forum in which they daily live and work, will be a bulwark of strength to others.

No one denies that the right to dissent is an inalienable right. But dissent has its boundaries. When dissent impinges upon the just rights of others, when dissent becomes destructive of the lawful claims of others, it has gone beyond its justifiable limits. Above all, when dissent sets itself up as doctrine, sustained in that position by self-styled theologians, and self-appointed interpreters of conciliar documents, then it must be recognized—and dealt with—for what it is, a perversion of truth.

To quote the most obvious example—the substitution of worldly clothing for the Holy Habit—Pope Paul is most explicit as to what he means by "experimenting" with a "modernized version" of religious dress. To the Mothers General his words are explicit and unmistakable:

> These appeals (for the modernization of Habits) have been diversely welcomed by your religious families: some have shown a certain mistrust in face of this aggiornamento in clothing, others have allowed themselves to be tempted to excessive "worldliness." My dear Daughters, it is not only the exterior Habit itself which influences and safeguards a true and authentic religious life. Certainly some modifications are necessary. Nevertheless, care should be taken to avoid extremes, so that the religious Habit, by its simplicity and its modesty always remain according to the standing tradition of the Church and the wise prescription of the Conciliar Decree: *Signum Consecrationis*—the sign of the state of life embraced by the consecrated virgin, recognizable to all.
>
> Audience of the Holy Father to the Mothers General
> Rome, March 7, 1967

A minority of Sisters and their vocal collaborators have taken the initiative in speaking against the religious life, alleging that the "Holy Spirit is opening new doors." The warnings of Pope

Paul VI against excesses should be a compelling motive for the majority to raise their voice and present their views with all the courage of a St. Michael protesting those who have declared, "I will not serve." If the wishes of the Church, rather than pious platitudes, are to be the living guidelines for Sisters in the contemporary world; if the Holy Father's words are listened to as having true authority, then every Sister must be wakened to the unlimited opportunities that are hers to render valiant service to the life she has embraced. The times demand the best and the most of every Sister to fight for what she truly believes in. No one is obliged to remain in the religious life if she feels she has somehow "outgrown" it—but no one has a right to spoil it for those who wish to live it according to the true interpretation (the Pope's) of the post-conciliar decrees. The more generously each Sister answers the demands now placed upon her, the more will her vision expand, and the greater will be her energy in "striving after the greater gifts . . . the more excellent way" (1 Cor. 12-31).

Neither human respect nor a natural diffidence should prevent a Sister from expressing her convictions, whether with members of her own community, with those of other communities, or with the laity. The latter, for the most part, need and eagerly accept the reassurances that only a Sister obedient to the Church and devoted to renewed religious life can give. As for her Sister associates, they may not immediately respond, even when they are interiorly heartened. To such a situation might be applied the element of surprise that the words of Christ give to the Last Judgment. "Then the just will answer him saying, 'Lord, when did we see You hungry and feed You, or thirsty, and give You to drink?' " Indeed, it may well be that the Sister who speaks out openly, sincerely and courageously, in favor of the essentials of the religious life, will reap here and now the result of her words and her attitude.

Sisters everywhere are humbly grateful when God uses them as instruments in attracting vocations to their Community. How much greater is the service rendered by a Sister who strengthens those who, having once answered the call to follow Christ, are now confused by other voices—voices that hold no note of the need for self-denial; voices that urge a refusal of the joy that can be found in following Christ poor, chaste and obedient as He manifested Himself in the Gospel!

This is a historic moment in the Church. It is a historic moment in the religious life. Intensive preparations are now in progress in every Community, preparatory for the mandated General Assemblies that will be held in 1968. Just as in the same year, the Presidential election will render every private citizen all-important to the cause, so in the year of a General Assembly, the views of the private Sisters will determine the issues. Under such circumstances, and especially in our unprecedented times, one might say that each Sister in a Community assumes the stature of a founder, since to preserve is, in a manner, to create anew. For its successful continuance, the religious life requires at this period both extensive pruning of its branches, and a wise and vigilant protection of its roots.

Mindful of her responsibility as "founder" each Sister will enter wholeheartedly into the preliminary plans for her Community's General Assembly. The *Norms for Implementing the Decree of Vatican II on Adaptation and Renewal of the Religious Life* clearly call for "free and extensive consultation of the members"—the results of which consultations are to be "correlated in a way that will help guide the chapter in its work." Privately and publicly, then, the Sisters will consult with one another. The foundation upon which each Sister should rest the strength and validity of her own views, she should also look for in the views of others. The questions each should ask of herself are: "Is this rule, is this practice, is this recommended attire meaningful within the framework of contemporary religious life?" "Are all suggestions in conformity with the Decrees of Vatican II?" And finally, and of tremendous importance, is the question: "Do these recommendations agree with the repeated public statements of Pope Paul VI?" For Peter is still the Rock—and on this rock, let us raise our voice and cast our vote for the future health and vigor of religious life in the Church.

Books and Published Articles
by Sister Bertrande Meyers, D.C.

BOOKS

The Education of Sisters. New York: Sheed and Ward, 1940
Then and Now. St. Louis: The Vincentian Press, 1946
Devotedly Yours. Chicago: Empire-Stone Press, 1950
A Woman Named Louise. Normandy, Missouri, Marillac College Press, 1956
Sisters for the 21st Century. New York: Sheed and Ward, 1965
Always Springtime. St. Louis: Marillac Towers Press, 1969

ARTICLES

"A Cause in Christ," *The Journal of Religious Instruction.* XIII (January, 1943) 338-50.
"Seven League Boots for Supervision," *Catholic High School Quarterly* Bulletin, II (January, 1944) 3-13.
"Problems the Child Brings to the School," *Proceedings of the Thirty-third National Conference of Catholic Charities* (New Orleans, Louisiana, 1947).
"How a Catholic Social Center Makes Its Contribution to Family Life through a Recreational Program for the Aging," *Proceedings of the Thirty-seventh National Conference of Catholic Charities* (1951) 173-178.
"Gray Hairs and Books," *The Catholic Library World* XXVII (November, 1955) 57-59.
Sisters in Social Work, Report of Everett Curriculum Workshop, (Everett, Washington, June 1 to August 30, 1956) 103-106.

"Today's Student—Tomorrow's Leader," *Hospital Progress* (August, 1956).

"How to Make the Religious Vocation Attractive," *Proceedings of the Tenth Annual Convocation of the Vocation Institute* (Notre Dame, Indiana, 1956) 82-95.

"Group Guidance in the Elementary School," *The Catholic Educational Review,* LV (February, 1957) 96-107.

"Oil for the Flickering Lamp," *The Catholic Nurse,* 5 (March, 1957) 28-35.

"Librarians and Nuns—Impressions vs. Portraits," *The Catholic Library World,* 28 (May, 1957) 387-393.

"Life's Golden Years Offer a Challenge," *The Benedictine Review,* XII (July, 1957) 23-30.

"The Place of Religious in Social Work," *Sister Formation Bulletin,* III (Summer, 1957) 1-8.

"Our Gripes—Let's Come to Grips with Them," *The Catholic Nurse,* VI (September, 1957) 45-52, 58-59.

"The Group Process in Education," *The Interprovincial Newsletter,* School Sisters of Notre Dame XXVIII (October, 1957) 13-20.

"The New Excellence," *Vital Speeches,* XXVI (June 15, 1960) 531-535.

"Four Stories of Flannery O'Connor," *Thought,* XXXVII (Autumn, 1962) 410-426.

Sister Bertrande was one of a large number who wrote "A Tribute" to Flannery O'Connor, *Esprit* (Winter 1964) 13-14.

"A Conflict in Color," *The Daughter of Charity,* I (Spring Issue, 1963) 13-14.

"Vanishing Sisters," *Ave Maria* (February 8, 1964) 5-7, 26-27.

Sister Bertrande was one of seven authorities familiar with Catholic Higher Education in this country to answer the queston: "What evidence of 'the fresh wind blowing through the Church' do you see in Catholic Colleges and Universities of America?" *The Critic* (December, 1963) 56-57, under the title "Prevailing Winds on the Catholic Campus."

"Qualifications of Tomorrow's Sisters," *The Theresian* (Summer, 1965) 4-5.

"Who Is Sick Among Us?" *Thought,* XLI (Autumn, 1966) 366-380.

"Sisters, Isn't It about Time?" *Ave Maria* 105 (March 4, 1967) 6-9, 27-28.

"Sisters and Pope Paul's Year of Faith," *Sisters Today,* 39 (February, 1968) 280-288.

"Fire, Flood, Earthquake—Sursum Corda, Sisters!" *Sisters Today,* 38 (June, 1967) 333-344.

"Raise Your Voice—Cast Your Vote," *Vital Speeches* (August 15, 1967) XXXIII, 661-664.

"Today's Candidate for the Religious Life," *Daughter of Charity,* 7 (Fall, 1968) 1-3.

"The Gift," *Daughter of Charity,* 7 (Winter, 1968-1969), (back cover) a poem.